SUFFRAGISTS AND LIBERALS

SUFFRAGISTS
AND LIBERALS

The Politics of Woman Suffrage in England

David Morgan

BASIL BLACKWELL · OXFORD · 1975

Set in Grotesque and Intertype Baskerville
Printed in Great Britain
by Western Printing Services Ltd, Bristol
and bound at The Kemp Hall Bindery, Oxford

Contents

To Sally

Preface

My debt to those who have written on Edwardian England is clear from the text. I greatly value the comments of my colleagues Dr. John Rowe and Dr. Patrick Buckland at Liverpool and of Professor Joe Banks now at Leicester. I am indebted to the staffs of the various libraries mentioned in the Bibliography—their courtesy and help made my task a much lighter one. Errors of fact or interpretation, of course, must lie solely at my door.

Every effort was made to trace the copyright of letters and other documents cited in this book. Where a copyright has been unwittingly infringed I hope the holder will accept my sincere apologies. For permission to quote from letters and documents I am grateful to the University of Birmingham, Miss Margaret Sinclair, Lord Aberconway, the Director of the First Beaverbrook Foundation, the Viscount Harcourt, the Hon. Mark Bonham Carter, Lord Aberdeen, Lord Selborne, the Trustees of the National Library of Scotland, the Librarian of the British Library of Political and Economic Science, Lord Samuel, the Controller of H.M. Stationery Office, the Director of the London Museum, the Librarian of the University of Newcastle Upon Tyne, the Clerk of the Records of the House of Lords, Earl Balfour, the Trustees of the National Library of Ireland, the Viscount Knollys, Sir William Gladstone, Bart., Professor Ann K. S. Lambton, Lord Gainford, Lord Long of Wraxall, William Heinemann Ltd., the Trustees of the Fawcett Library, Lord Henderson, the Hon. Edward Carson, Miss Evamaria Brailsford, the National Liberal Agents Association, Lady Katherine Oldfield, and Lady Frances Ferguson.

I. Introduction

Edwardian England witnessed much political turmoil and not a
little hysteria. Ministers by 1910 had accepted greatly curtailed
schedules of public appearances and had come to accept with
gratitude the extensive security precautions which daily sur-
rounded them. By 1912 there was gossip that assassinations were
being planned against the Prime Minister, Herbert Asquith, and
the Chancellor of the Exchequer, David Lloyd George. The
former—it was claimed—had narrowly been missed by a hatchet
flung into his carriage in Dublin. The latter had had his new
house-to-be partly destroyed by fire. The supposed assassins were
never found but, in the case of both assaults, arrests were made.
The culprits in both cases were women who claimed that their
actions were a direct consequence of the Liberal government's
refusal to grant or allow the parliamentary vote to be given
to women. Edwardian England rang with the cry 'Votes for
Women!' and the campaign for those votes contributed not a
little to the turmoil visible in the years before 1914.

This book is a study of that campaign as it entered its climacteric phase and failed. It is not a study of feminism as such. That
would call for an interdisciplinary effort and would, almost certainly, need a comparative, international dimension adequately to
cope with so large and diversified a subject. This study, further,
does not have for its focus the *whole* campaign for what was called
Woman Suffrage. Several studies already exist which give an
adequate framework to the total picture[1] and these are well

[1] Notable general studies are Roger Fulford, *Votes for Women, The
Story of a Struggle* (Faber, London, 1958). Constance Rover, *Women's
Suffrage and Party Politics in Britain 1866–1914* (Routledge, London,
1967). See Bibliography.

Introduction

supplemented by parts of the memoirs of participants or studies of
Suffrage leaders.[2] Both in turn provide essential material for
studies of individual or small groups of Suffragists—as they were
called—which are illuminating not only for feminism, but for the
Victorian and Edwardian epochs.

At the primary source level printed sources in general, and
Suffragist sources in particular, are relatively good—the Suffragists being prolific pamphleteers and magazine contributors.[3] Unprinted sources for the nineteenth century and early twentieth
century are, of course, generally not thin and are voluminous
for the Edwardian period.[4] Suffragist unprinted sources are dis-
appointingly sparse. What survived police raids, self-destruction, a
Thames flood in 1919, among Mrs. Emmeline Pankhurst's
Women's Social and Political Union papers is held in the London
Museum. A relatively tiny corpus of letters of Mrs. Fawcett, the
President of the leading Suffrage society—the National Union of
Women's Suffrage Societies—is held in the Fawcett Society
Library in London which also houses an immense collection of
books on feminism and the activities of women all over the world.

Most studies whether of the whole campaign, or of organizations and leaders within it, have focused, perhaps inevitably, on
the Suffragists themselves—their motivation, experiences, knowledge, organizing and campaigning abilities, and particularly on
their views of their dealings with party politicians. With one
exception no sustained effort, at the level of primary sources, has

[2] Many of these exist, e.g. Millicent Fawcett, *The Women's Victory and
After. Personal Reminiscences 1911–18* (Sidgwick and Jackson, London,
1920). Christabel Pankhurst, *Unshackled. The Story of How We Won The
Vote* (Hutchinson, London, 1959). Emmeline Pankhurst, *My Own Story*
(Eveleigh Nash, London, 1914). Again, David Mitchell, *The Fighting
Pankhursts. A Study in Tenacity* (Jonathan Cape, London, 1967). But see
Bibliography.

[3] The main Suffrage organizations went into publishing and brought out
numbers of pamphlets, some of which survive in a collection at the
Fawcett Society Library, London. See Bibliography.

[4] Examples are the Asquith Papers at the Bodleian Library, Oxford, the
Campbell-Bannerman and Herbert Gladstone Papers at the British
Museum, and the Lloyd George and Bonar Law Papers at the Beaverbrook
Library, London. See Bibliography.

been made to comprehend the perceptions of leading politicians and, in particular, ministers. Much use has been made of Hansard but not of cabinet papers and private letters in which realities implicit in public statements—in and out of Parliament—are made explicit, or again, in which an illuminating scrawled aside throws floods of light on the meaning the writer is actually giving to his own words. A rounded view of how politicians saw Woman Suffrage has thus not been given—if only because no one, it seems, has looked at their papers with this in mind.

The campaign then has been written up as though the politicians were a static 'given'. Since the bulk of the writing was done by Suffragist leaders or their admirers this is not surprising, though it is fair to add that, during the campaign, those leaders were fairly well informed on the changing position of Woman Suffrage at cabinet level and framed their tactics accordingly. As an issue Woman Suffrage was not a bone of contention *between* the political parties after 1906 and, as such, has received relatively little attention from professional historians. Recent studies of Edwardian Liberalism are, inevitably, focused on the problem of explaining the rise of the Labour party. Dr. Emy's analysis[5] of the 'new' social politics makes clear, if only by silence, how little benefit his 'new' Liberals saw in enfranchising and mobilizing women for their causes. Dr. Mathew's study of the Liberal Imperialists prior to 1905[6] reveals that Asquith felt that the Liberal party did not stand to gain by further franchise extension and it is precisely for standing by this view in regard to Woman Suffrage that Dr. Clarke most faults Asquith's subsequent leadership.[7] Neither of the two studies of the Liberals after 1906 examines either the evolution of the Suffrage question or its interaction with other problems.

Earlier accounts of the period are not much more illuminating.

[5] Emy, H. V., *Liberals, Radicals and Social Politics 1892–1914* (Cambridge U.P., 1973).

[6] Mathew, H. G. C., *The Liberal Imperialists. The ideas and politics of a post-Gladstonian élite* (Oxford U.P., 1973).

[7] Clarke, P. F., *Lancashire and the New Liberalism* (Cambridge U.P., 1973), p. 389.

Introduction

Where the consideration of Suffrage has been more than perfunctory the emphasis has been on the significance of the campaign among women rather than for Parliament and party leaderships. Thus, on the question of whether militancy actually destroyed the chance of securing some Woman Suffrage bill before 1914, most authors are inclined to affirm that it did while producing little evidence for this view. Ensor admits that at first militancy stimulated the campaign, but goes on to affirm how later 'the hostilities which it aroused set the clock back'.[8] Halevy argued that a 'military concept of government'[9] probably lay at the base of both government and public opposition—a belief that men, who ultimately defend states, should ultimately rule them. On this analysis one would have expected that Edwardian domestic unrest and military insecurity would have reinforced this attitude. Nevertheless, Halevy later seems to imply that in 1912–13 there was a chance, military conception of government notwithstanding, that some Suffrage bill could be secured and that militancy ruined this by alienating ministers such as Lloyd George. He then goes on, however, to weaken this point by noting the machinations of Asquith among the Irish and Liberals, and ends by noting that Suffrage was in a 'vicious cycle' of the government's making.[10] In short, while Ensor is clear cut on Suffrage and militancy, Halevy veers between affirming that, on the one hand, Suffrage was never a possibility and that, on the other hand, it was foiled because of militancy, or Asquith, or fate, or all three.

No such confusion is visible in Dangerfield's brilliantly evocative essay.[11] The melodrama of the campaign after 1906 is well captured with Christabel Pankhurst in the role of the personally unattractive heroine, and Asquith in that of the not unattractive though devious villain. The militant campaign—a 'revolt' for

[8] Ensor, R. C. K. *England 1870–1914* (Oxford History of England, in 14 vols.), (The Clarendon Press, Oxford), Vol. 14, 1952, p. 398.

[9] Halevy, Elie, *The Rule of Democracy 1905–14* (A History of the English People in the Nineteenth Century, in 6 vols.), Vol. 6, Book II (Ernest Benn Ltd., London, 1952), p. 513.   [10] *Ibid.*, pp. 522–4.

[11] Dangerfield, George, *The Strange Death of Liberal England* (Paladin, London, 1966).

4

Halevy—was for Dangerfield a rebellion against security and respectability, a movement 'from death into life'.[12] Facing it was a moribund Liberalism which, as the deviousness of its leader proclaimed, did not deserve to survive. Far from being counter-productive militancy made the Suffrage movement a political success. In June 1914 did not Asquith bow on Suffrage to 'some unconscious and almost unimaginable prompting of the whole people?' and had not militancy called this forth?[13] An obdurate Christabel Pankhurst and a determined Mr. Asquith were, seemingly, both the products of a society in the grip of a Fronde, the death throes in fact of Liberal England. For Dangerfield the militants were at one with working-class and Tory extremists— both seemed to be seeking not victory for their beliefs so much as battle itself. Mrs. Pankhurst, desperately seeking her niche in History, was the symbol for Dangerfield of the striving of women, not so much to be equal, but to be free to create their own roles, to assert their dormant masculinity. Asquith, uncomprehending and blinkered, symbolized an old order fast passing away. Overarching both was the mysterious zeitgeist, the spirit of the age which was only glimpsed in the actions and utterances of its more frenetic actors.

Such levels of generalization are barely susceptible to historical proof or disproof, and the evidence for Edwardian England is probably insufficient to determine the question finally. Dangerfield provided a brilliant description of the consequences of the clash of ideologies and the book did not seek to be a rigorous analysis of behaviour as such. If one descends from the former level to that of the actual and changing perceptions of the key actors involved, and the interrelatedness of political questions before 1914, then the dynamics in the situation can be revealed and it may be possible to escape from presenting a static portrait of ideologies, feminist and masculine, in conflict. Between the 'heroic' tradition of feminist memoirs and studies and the zeitgeist approach of Dangerfield, a course can be steered which will reveal both motifs as components of a very much more complex process of interaction.

[12] *Ibid. p.* 136.   [13] *Ibid.*, p. 331.

Something of the kind has already been attempted in a study by Constance Rover.[14] Her concern, however, was not specifically with the climacteric of the Suffrage campaign after 1906 and she relied too heavily on an analysis of the *public* utterances of politicians and Suffragists. Again, she missed the critical effect on the Suffrage question of other issues at particular times and the structured situation in which the Liberal party found itself as time passed. She was clear that Asquith and not militancy ruined any chance of success prior to 1914 though she offered little first-class evidence for this conviction. She saw 1910–11 as the best period and argued that 'After 1912 the time was no longer ripe.'[15] In fact precisely the opposite was probably the case and even then Asquith's opposition made success unlikely. The whole point about Suffrage was that Liberals were concerned about much that needed reform in the area of franchise qualifications and registration and could not agree on what share of their concern Suffrage should have. On top of this were their many other political convictions, an awkward parliamentary situation, and the inherent difficulties involved in timing franchise legislation. Only clear strong leadership from the cabinet could have overcome the difficulties and it is precisely at this point that Asquith's personal hostility is so crucial. There is need, therefore, to elucidate the changing political context in which the Woman Suffrage campaign took place after 1906.

We must, however, begin with the origins and development of the Suffrage movement and its arrival by 1906 at a position from which it could, with some force, demand the extension of the parliamentary vote to women. The economic, educational and legal changes in the nineteenth century had, cumulatively, provided a mass of women who could be appealed to by an organized, feminist elite. We need to be clear how this elite assessed its overall position and latent strength and why the incoming Liberal government seemed to it to present a most favourable opportunity for a successful campaign.

Equally it must be made clear why, seen from within the Liberal

[14] Rover, Constance, *op. cit.*   [15] *Ibid.*, p. 195.

leadership, this expectation was ill founded. We need to see Woman Suffrage as a cause and movement from the perspective of party leaders who saw themselves facing a range of possible alternatives once they took office and saw, too, many obstacles to the achieving of any coherent Liberal programme. We will not grasp their reactions to the violent campaign mounted against them after 1906 unless we hold in mind that in part they regarded that campaign as the sudden effusion into the political arena of a question which had not been, in any real sense, before the country and must therefore take its place in a long queue.

Expectations of such a deeply contradictory character were the ground of the fury and frustration of both sides in the years after 1906. The record of this is analysed in three chapters up to August 1911 and the passage of the Parliament Act, a critical watershed for any Woman Suffrage hopes. With that behind them Suffragists—the term they used—looked expectantly for success; and, in four further chapters, there follows an analysis, first of their possible success had not chance intervened, then of their failure and finally, under the impact of World War I, their partial success in 1918. The interaction of party politics and crises in leadership, of major war and desperate efforts to mobilize for it, also form part of this narrative. By 1917 Lloyd George, a Liberal Prime Minister of a coalition government, was able to use many Tory and Labour votes to secure passage of a bill which neither cared for; to use a war situation in fact to forge the bipartisan front necessary to pass the measure and enfranchise women.

Suffrage thus came in from the periphery of politics in 1906 to the edge of its centre by 1912, receded, and was then carried back in 1916–17 by the momentum of events skilfully manipulated by the Prime Minister. The final campaign throws light on Suffragists and the Liberals in Parliament and cabinet. It also illuminates the Liberal party and the complex political process of the period.

II. The Movement and its Origins

*Men, as well as women, do not need political
rights in order that they may govern, but in
order that they may not be misgoverned.*
J. S. Mill, 1861.[1]

The demand for Woman Suffrage in 1906 was the end product
of a campaign at least forty years old. By that date the formula-
tion 'Woman Suffrage' connoted in the first place the National
Union of Women's Suffrage Societies, a federation of local
societies seeking the parliamentary vote for women. It also connoted a very new organization, the Women's Social and Political
Union, founded in 1903 in Manchester and fast gaining converts
in London. At another level the term connoted more widely a
movement, a body of ideas, a cause, allegiance to which, in whole
or part, was much wider than organizational membership. The
cause may be termed feminism, and its long-sought goal was the
liberation of women from male-determined roles. It attacked an
education and upbringing aimed solely at a wife/mother role
and sought a *choice* of roles in life for women. Not all Suffragists
were ardent feminists by any means—but where the parliamentary vote and full political participation was demanded *by* women
for women, the rationale owed most of its coherence to feminist
roots.

The origins and nineteenth-century development of the feminist
movement in general, and Woman Suffrage organizations in
particular, need no comprehensive recounting here. It is, however, necessary to draw attention to aspects of that history firstly

[1] Quoted in Rover, Constance, *op. cit.*, p. 34.

8

to illuminate the situation of the Suffrage campaign after 1900 and, secondly, to reveal the grounds both of optimism and anxiety among its adherents. We will not understand the explosion after 1906 unless we bear in mind that those involved were acutely conscious that their hour was at hand.

An organization devoting itself to political participation for women and able to show a continuous history must be held to date from the rejection of the efforts of women to be included in the 1867 Reform Bill. A coherent case for feminine participation in politics and public life went back two generations before that date. The intellectual ferment associated with the French Revolution, perhaps inevitably, produced a spokeswoman for feminism in England and the yeast of feminine discontent permeated subsequent movements of ideas. Feminism, after the 1780s, was a question that most social and political thinkers were aware of even if they disdained or disregarded *feminists.*

The spokeswoman in the 1790s was Mary Wollstonecraft in her *Vindication of the Rights of Women.*[2] Spurred to anger by Burke's *Reflections on the French Revolution,* she had written a *Vindication of the Rights of Man* in reply. Spurred to even greater anger by her friend Tom Paine's *Rights of Man* she penned her trenchant *Vindication* in reply, employing most of the arguments used against the prescriptive rights of kings against that king among women, Man. Woman, she argued, the captive creature of man, would prevent him attaining his full liberty. Not until there was a revolution *between* the sexes would man —and woman—be truly free. It was an argument which was to be much used. Among Socialist thinkers William Godwin, Saint-Simon and Owen were to take up the point though there was not then or later a socialist consensus on it. The Utilitarians in England were divided, too, in the 1820s. James Mill in his article on government in the 1824 Supplement to the *Britannica* held that as dependants women were represented via fathers or

[2] Mary Wollstonecraft, *A Vindication of the Rights of Women* (Walter Scott, London, 1891).

husbands. Bentham, however, dissented from this view. Even more strongly put was the rejoinder to Mill from the socialist William Thompson, whose *Appeal of one half of the human race* ... (in 1825)[3] was an impassioned rejection of this dependent status for women.

A case, however, was one thing, an organization another. The agitation for a Reform bill in the 1820s and the Chartist movement in the 1830s produced feminist incidents but no organization. As the agitation for a Reform bill reached a crescendo in Parliament 'Orator' Hunt—an advocate of universal suffrage—presented to that body the petition of Miss Mary Smith which sought the vote for unmarried, qualified women. It was this which forced the parliamentary draftsmen to qualify references to 'person' by the adjective 'male'—for the first time in such legislation. When this same language was used in the Municipal Corporation Act of 1835 it had the effect of denying such women a right they had—technically—been allowed to exercise in the older boroughs.

Accompanying specifically political agitation in the 30s and 40s was the appearance of women novelists. Besides the obvious George Eliot there were polemicists such as Mrs. William Ellis who was not really a feminist writer, and Harriet Martineau and Lady Morgan who were. In 1847 Mrs. Anne Knight, a Quaker, published the first recognizable Woman Suffrage pamphlet as the Chartist agitation was subsiding. Women had been active in the Corn Law League, especially in Manchester. In 1851 a Sheffield Association for Female Suffrage was formed and produced a Suffrage petition which Lord Carlisle presented to the Lords.

The fifties, in fact, proved to be a fruitful prelude to attempts at organizations. In 1850 what later became known in Suffrage circles as Brougham's Act declared, *inter alia*, that 'in all Acts,

[3] William Thompson, *An appeal on behalf of one half of the human race, women, against the pretensions of the other half, men, to retain them in political and thence in civil and domestic slavery* (Longmans, Hurst Rees, London, 1825).

words importing the masculine gender shall be deemed and taken to include females, unless the contrary be expressly provided'. The Crimean War provided in Florence Nightingale a well publicized symbol of heroic, practical womanhood. Behind this lay educational activity at the Governesses' Benevolent Institute, reconstituted into Queen's College London after 1848. Four of the leaders of this activity founded in 1858 the *Englishwoman's Journal* and the Society for the Employment of Women.[4] If the former came to symbolize hope the latter was eloquent of the distress suffered by middle-class women compelled to earn their own livelihood.

The Endowed Schools Royal Commission of 1862–4 and the involvement of feminists in its concerns gave feminists a focus for activity. In the autumn of 1865 J. S. Mill, publicly canvassed for by Madame Bodichon, was elected M.P. for Westminster. Later that year Lord Palmerston, the Prime Minister, who was hostile to reform, died and was succeeded by Earl Russell, with Gladstone leading in the Commons. The subsequent events leading to the Reform Act of 1867 were vitally important first in the rising and then the dashing of Suffrage hopes—the event which launched an ongoing organization. In March 1866 the Liberal government introduced its bill which split the party and ushered in the Conservatives by June. That same month Mill presented a petition for Suffrage with 1,400 signatures, more than Suffragists had ever dreamt of before and comprising a roster of prominent Victorian women writers and intellectuals. In the autumn of 1866, following a lecture by Madame Bodichon in Manchester, a Manchester Woman Suffrage committee was formed with Miss Lydia Becker[5] as Secretary and numbering among its members the influential local Radicals Dr. Richard Pankhurst and Mr. Jacob Bright.

Months earlier, when the Liberals had introduced their bill,

---

[4] The four were Jessie Boucherette 1825–1905, Elizabeth Garret 1836–1917, Barbara Bodichon 1827–91 and Adelaide Proctor 1825–64.

[5] Lydia Becker—1827–90—daughter of a Manchester calico printer. A botanist, Editor *Women's Suffrage Journal* 1870–90.

Disraeli had said 'that in a country governed by a woman—when you allow women to form part of the other estate of the realm—peeresses in their own right for example . . . I do not see . . . on what reasons . . . she has not the right to vote'. By May of 1867, when his own bill was challenged by Mill on Suffrage, the Prime Minister was somewhat less forthcoming. In the light of the 1850 Act Mill sought to remove the word 'man' from the text and insert 'person' so as to include women under its provisions. In the event 73 M.P.s voted for the amendment, including in this number such men as John Bright, Henry Labouchere and the Christian Socialist, Tom Hughes. Opposed were 194 M.P.s numbering among them, significantly for the future, W. E. Gladstone. Mill's reaction was that such a vote gave 'an immense impetus to the question'.

If not immense, the impetus was at least sufficient to make the provisional Suffrage committees into permanent organizations in Manchester, London, Edinburgh and, in 1868, to establish the National Society for Woman Suffrage. That same year the Reform Act was tested by women householders who sought to register and vote under it. All rested their case on the fact that the 1867 Act, in its ratepaying clauses, used the masculine gender throughout, and had no express provision excluding women. The Court of Common Pleas rejected the application.[6] *The Times* had not failed to point out in advance the rejection would mean that the country was 'formally, and in the light of day, committing itself through its judicial tribunal to the dangerous doctrine that representation need not go along with taxation'. The point did not go unnoticed. Some months later Jacob Bright, seeking a restoration of the municipal franchise, 'somewhat to his own surprise, found himself suported by the Government of the day'.[7]

By 1869, then, women as householders might exercise the

[6] Chorlton *v.* Lings L. R. 4 C.P. 374 (1868).

[7] Quoted from Metcalfe, A. E., *Woman's Effort* (B. H. Blackwell, Oxford, 1917), p. 6. J. S. Mill at this time published his essay *The Subjection of Women*, a work which was long to be cited both for and against Suffrage.

municipal franchise. Not, however, if they were married since, being in the legal state of 'coverture', their property was deemed to be represented by their husbands. The fact that this state was soon modified in the Married Women's Property Act of 1870, which gave married women possession of their own earnings, did not prevent a hostile ruling which debarred them from voting.[8] This legal counter attack was the prelude to dissension in the Suffrage movement. The issue of coverture divided spinsters and widows from married Suffragists, while the general acceptance by many Suffragists of the 1867 Act, despite its exclusion of women, was a cause of further friction. The defeat of Jacob Bright at the 1874 General Election was the trigger of dissension. Lydia Becker, the energetic Manchester spinster Secretary of the National Society, seeking a sponsor for the Society's bill, accepted a Tory, William Forsyth, M.P. for Marylebone, who amended it by adding a clause 'that nothing in this Act shall make women under coverture eligible to register and vote'. Using London support Becker carried this amendment through her Executive and membership.

In the event Gladstone himself led the opposition to the bill, revealing for all to see the gulf that existed between himself and Suffragists who were, in fact, predominantly Liberals. The return of Disraeli was of no help though, between 1876 and 1879, with Jacob Bright back in the Commons, the coverture clause was removed.

The return of the Liberals, albeit under Gladstone, raised hopes of another Reform bill though among Suffragists there was caution. In the event the Prime Minister was adamant. Referring to the bill, and arguing that Woman Suffrage should be 'dissociated from every notion of Party . . .', he went on 'The cargo which the vessel carries is, in our opinion, a cargo as large as she can carry safely.'[9] Gladstone's own Postmaster-General—the blind ex-Professor of Political Economy at Cambridge, Henry Fawcett —would have earlier privately indicated this opinion to his wife

[8] Regina *v.* Harald L. R. 7 Q.B., 361 (1872).
[9] Quoted in Rover, Constance, *op. cit.*, p. 118.

who was a prominent Suffragist.[10] She, like Lydia Becker, was not over anxious to press Gladstone too hard so that the larger bill would be endangered. It was not only coverture but party loyalties which could split Suffragists—Liberal women were still Liberals, first and foremost.

Events in the 80s were to politicize women more widely than ever before. The Corrupt Practices Act of 1883, by its ban on paid election canvassers, had led both parties to establish women's auxiliary organizations—the Primrose League in 1885, and the Women's Liberal Federation and Women's Liberal Unionist Federation in 1887. These absorbed many Suffragists but at first proved difficult ground for Suffragist propaganda. Feminism in the 80s and 90s was still too *avant-garde* even for the bulk of women political activists. Two causes, however, were making it less so yearly. The first was the growth of the Temperance movement. The second was the campaign against legalized prostitution in England, led by Josephine Butler,[11] which sought the repeal of the Contagious Diseases Acts. In the 70s Mrs. Butler had helped divide Suffragists by this campaign, since many feared that the feminist cause would be identified with it and its 'daring' focus of concern. The campaign led to a Royal Commission on the White Slave Traffic. In 1883 a Commons resolution favourable to repeal was passed and in 1885 W. T. Stead, in a series of sensational articles in the *Pall Mall Gazette*, had publicly ventilated the whole question. The bringing of prostitution into lively public debate had not a little to do with the subsequent endorsing of Woman Suffrage by organizations such as the Primrose League and the potent Woman's Christian Temperance Union, which had been opposed to or sceptical of its propriety and value.

By the late 1880s, most of the arguments for and against Suffrage in principle and practice which were to be used

[10] Dame Millicent Fawcett 1847–1929—married Henry Fawcett in 1867 when he was M.P. for Brighton. Active in Vigilance Society after 1885. A Liberal Unionist from 1887 until she left them in 1903 over free trade. President of NUWSS through the Suffrage campaign.

[11] Josephine Butler 1828–1906. Secretary of the Ladies National Association for Repeal of the Contagious Diseases Acts.

until 1918 were already stock.[12] Suffragists used a variety of approaches. They claimed the vote for qualified unmarried women and widows by pointing to the fact that no man as such represented them and hence they were unrepresented taxpayers who, prior to the 1832 Act, might technically have claimed the right to vote. More generally, for working-class women they claimed the vote as a means of self-protection in a hard, competitive, exploiting world; for middle-class women they asserted the vote would open the doors of career opportunity. On the principle of an end to sex discrimination Suffragists claimed that women were entitled to, and needed, the recognition of full adult status and the responsibilities which went with it. Society, they claimed, would be the better for ceasing to treat large numbers of adults as minors.

Equally stock by the 1880s were the anti-Suffrage arguments. Women, the antis claimed, did not want the vote, preferring to rely on their husbands, fathers or other relatives to protect their interests. Women, again it was claimed, by reason of upbringing and temperament, were unsuited to comprehend or to soil themselves in the hurly-burly of the political world. Moreover, claimed opponents, was not voting a substitute for forcible settling of political arguments? Would a majority of men tolerate being out-voted by a minority of men added to a majority of women? A variant of this took the form of being concerned at a possible numerical superiority of women voters, and this at the centre of the world's greatest empire.

Some of these arguments lost their potency as the Suffrage claim was made in changing political circumstances. By the final campaign after 1906, for example, some women had had the municipal vote for a generation and had not shown themselves noticeably more unfit than male voters. Again, after 1906, the unrepresented taxpayer argument lost some of its force in a situation where the Liberal cabinet was actively debating Manhood Suffrage and was facing Labour and Radical demands

[12] For a full discussion of the arguments in the nineteenth century see Rover, Constance, *op. cit.*, Chaps. 4 and 5.

for Adult Suffrage. Nevertheless, each Suffrage debate in the Commons continued to have the full panoply of arguments arrayed on each side of the question.

In 1888 the Unionists passed the Local Government Act which created the County Councils. In London three women—Lady Sandhurst, Miss Cobden and Miss Cons—were elected to the London County Council. The elections were contested and, in the Lords, it was ruled that for women the right to vote did not involve the right to sit.[13] Before the ruling had been handed down there had, in fact, occurred a split in the National Society. In 1889 the Executive persisted in retaining the coverture clause and in consequence the dissidents—including Dr. and Mrs. Pankhurst, Elizabeth Wolstenholme Elmy, Josephine Butler, Mr. and Mrs. Jacob Bright, and Elizabeth Cady Stanton and William Lloyd Garrison, two pioneer feminists from the United States—withdrew and formed the Women's Franchise League. It adopted an earlier Suffrage bill, drafted by Dr. Pankhurst, which ignored coverture for qualified women. Further, the bill had a clause declaring that no person should be disqualified for election or appointment to any office on grounds of sex or marriage. Significantly, meetings of the League ended with a resolution that 'This meeting resolves itself into a lobbying committee' after the passage of which the more zealous members left for the Commons to lobby M.P.s. After 1906 the same Dr. Pankhurst's wife was to play this scene for all—and more—than it was worth. R. B. Haldane and Edward Grey who were both to be ministers after 1906 had promised to sponsor the bill. Haldane told Mrs. Pankhurst at the time that it was 'a declaration of principle' and would take fifty years to enact. She was to make him remember that reply.

Frustration with Liberalism in the 90s led the Pankhursts off into the newly formed Independent Labour party, and Dr. Pankhurst was an Independent Labour party candidate at Gorton, Manchester in 1895. A year earlier coverture had ceased to be an issue affecting propertied women and hence a cause of dis-

[13] De Sousa *v.* Cobden 1 Q.B., p. 687, Apr. 1891.

sension among Suffragists. Bruce McLaren, brother-in-law of
John Bright, had been instrumental in securing, in the 1894
Local Government Act, the right of married women to vote and
sit if they possessed a separate qualification from that of their
husbands.[14]

In 1897 the remnants of the 1889 split—sixteen societies in
all—came together to found the National Union of Women's
Suffrage Societies, which was united on the demand for Suffrage,
'as it is, and may be given to men'. This was a demand, in
effect, for the parliamentary franchise for those on the Local
Government Register and reflected the gains won up to that time.
Significantly, the union aimed at placing the Suffrage question,
'in such a position that no Government, of whatever party . . .
[should] . . . be able to touch the questions relating to representation, without at the same time removing the electoral disabilities
of women'. This is a neat summary of the standing of the Suffrage
cause in the 1890s. The three Reform Bills had left a great deal of
unfinished business in the realm of the franchise—business which,
as time passed, became more pressing for the Liberal party.
Suffragists sought to ensure that when the time came to deal with
the business their cause would be included in it—by whatever
party then in power. In the case of the Liberals it was clear that
the Lords would prove an obstruction to their proposals. On this,
one Suffragist at least, the Countess of Carlisle, President of the
Women's Liberal Federation and a Temperance leader was reso-
lute—'The action of the House of Lords throughout the last three
years, has brought home to the people the necessity of clearing
out of the way this ancient obstruction to all democratic reform,
an hereditary chamber.'[15]

Well might the Countess be so positive. More than any other
woman she had been responsible for making the Women's
Liberal Federation a power for Suffrage. The dispute over the

[14] In London this called for a new Act—the London County Council
Election Qualification Act of 1900.
[15] Pamphlet. The Countess of Carlisle, *Appeal by the Countess of
Carlisle* (Women's Liberal Federation, July 1895).

issue within the Federation had come into the open when she had joined the Executive Committee and, within two years, there had been a secession of those who feared or refused to take a strong Suffrage position.[16] In 1893 Object II of the Federation was changed from the 'protection of women and children', to the promotion of 'just legislation for women, including Local and Parliamentary franchise for all women on the same terms as men, and the removal of their legal disabilities'.[17] Thereafter the controversy was concentrated on the question of whether the Federation could support anti-Suffragists as official Liberal candidates. By 1902, at the sixteenth Annual Council of the Federation, the issue—which of course directly affected its position *vis-à-vis* the party—was resolved along the lines that, while local Associations might dissent, the Federation as a whole could not endorse such candidates. The involvement of Woman Suffrage with the larger questions of franchise changes desired by Liberals—a serious problem for Liberal women and Suffragists after 1906—was testified to by a further resolution endorsing 'one person, one vote'. For Suffrage this Council was a milestone. Whatever Suffragists might later think of pre-election pledges, the fact that a great majority of Liberals came back in 1906 privately pledged to favour Suffrage could not be an unimportant consideration for Liberal ministers.

Symptomatic of its growing strength and new-found unity—however fissured—was the internationalizing of the movement. In America, at the 1902 Convention of the National American Woman Suffrage Association, the President, Mrs. C. C. Catt, had led the way in establishing a temporary committee to plan for the founding of an international Suffrage organization at the coming 1904 Congress of the International Council of Women, to be held in Berlin. Preparations were put in hand and in 1904, as hoped, the International Woman Suffrage Alliance was established with

[16] The defectors helped establish the National Liberal Federation which did not fully endorse Suffrage until 1915.
[17] Pamphlet. Mrs. Eva MacLaren, *The History of Woman Suffrage in the Women's Liberal Federation* (Women's Lib. Fed., Apr. 1903).

the American pioneer Susan B. Anthony as its Honarary President, and Mrs. Catt of the U.S.A. and Mrs. Fawcett, the English President, as its President and Vice-President respectively. Eight countries had full delegations—Australia, Denmark, Germany, Great Britain, Netherlands, Norway, Sweden and America—while Austria, Finland, and Hungary were promised membership once their national organizations were properly organized. The Suffrage movement had been internationalized. Delegates to both the International Council of Women, and its Suffrage offshoot, were received by the German Empress, entertained by Chancellor von Bulow, and feted by the City of Berlin.

Originating in the revolutionary ferment of the late eighteenth century, continued and developed in Radical and Socialist circles in the nineteenth, toyed with by some English conservatives, Woman Suffrage had, by 1905, become embodied in England in a movement well placed to exploit political opportunity should it present itself and, potentially, capable of mobilizing a mass of women. To see why this was so we need to remember that educational and legal changes had already gone some way to liberating middle-class women. After 1900 it seemed that economic developments promised them a growing potential following.

Feminists in nineteenth-century England had been concerned with the various efforts to expand and transform educational opportunities for women—to move away from 'cultivation' to education.[18] The years after 1870 had, in this respect, seen a steady expansion of the role of the state in primary education and a constant growth in the number of schools based on the model of the North London Collegiate School (31 by 1901) and that of Cheltenham Ladies College (80 by 1890). Both pioneer institutions were identified with women—Miss Frances Buss and Miss Dorothea Beale—who acknowledged feminist career aspirations, even if they did not wholly share the desire for political participation. By the 1880s both Oxford and Cambridge universities had

[18] For a full discussion of the role of feminists in the changing education of women see Kamm, Josephine, *Hope Deferred* (Methuen, London, 1965).

institutions preparing women students for degrees, while the newly established civic universities imposed no bars on women entrants. Feminists, as such, could not claim to have been solely responsible for these developments. Feminist agitation, however, did contribute to a changed climate of opinion in which the education of girls was taken increasingly seriously, and in which pioneering efforts were made to develop different syllabi incorporating such 'new' subjects as History, Geography and English.

Equally, feminists had contributed to a change in the climate of opinion in the realm of the laws governing the rights of the women after marriage. In relation to their property the milestone had been the Married Women's Property Act of 1883. This gave to women married after that year sole power of disposition of their real and personal property, and similar power over property acquired after 1882 to those already married. This extended to all property owned by a married woman the right to its sole disposition given in 1870 to earnings, savings, stocks etc. Married women, despite these legal gains, continued to enjoy the benefits of coverture in one respect: namely, they were not liable for their debts. In other respects however—the law of divorce after 1857, guardianship of children after 1886, sex relations[19]—the legal position of married women remained a source of discontent for feminists[20] and was to continue to be so well into the twentieth century.

The advances which were made owed more to other factors, for example to the desire of fathers and trustees to protect property against marital 'adventurers' or bankruptcy, than to feminists as such. The law in any event was only infrequently relevant to the mass of women—working or not. Their lives were bounded as much as ever by family considerations and, if young, by expectations of marriage. The small surplus of women in the

[19] Regina *v.* Clarence 1888 22 Q.B.D., 23. In this case a wife who continued to cohabit with her husband was taken as assenting to intercourse.

[20] Regina *v.* Jackson 1891 1 Q.B., 671. This took away the husband's right to use reasonable force on, or to confine, his wife. He could no longer, in the words of Justice McCardie, treat his wife 'as he would a recalcitrant animal'.

population in general—and in the marriageable age groups—
continued to grow.[21] It was clear that spinsterhood faced a small
but growing number of women who must look for work to maintain themselves. This fact, plus their experience at work if they
could find employment, could not but help shape their view of
themselves and their needs.

The changing British economy was providing ever growing
numbers of women whose economic situation was both new and
often precarious. The woman worker was no new phenomenon
by 1900, having provided over a third of the total workforce since
the mid-century. What was new was that more and more women
were being pulled into a greater variety of jobs. The non-domestic
service sector of the economy was rapidly expanding. What has
been termed the 'typewriter, telephone, department store' revolution was visibly under way after 1900, absorbing thousands of
new women workers annually. By 1914 there were more than
half a million women at work in shops and offices. Parallel with
this went an expansion of the teaching and nursing professions so
that by 1914 nearly a quarter of a million women were so engaged. The continuous expansion of this service sector, allied to
the steady growth in numbers of women in the more traditional
areas such as textiles, clothing and food processing *plus* the slow
decline in entry into domestic service meant that the typical
woman worker was ceasing to be a domestic servant. Equally, as
a worker, she was slowly ceasing to be unorganized. Trade Union
membership among women tripled between 1900 and 1914,
rising to a figure of 437,000.[22] The change was far more than
simply quantitative. Women were prominent in the shorter hours
agitation in textiles and later in the shop steward movement.[23]

[21] Females per 1,000 males in 1851 numbered 1,042. By 1901 this was
1,068.

[22] Mitchell, B. R., and Deane, P., *Abstract of British Historical Statistics*
(Cambridge U.P., 1962), p. 68.

[23] See Hutchins, B. L., *Women in Modern Industry* (G. Bell and Sons,
London, 1915), pp. 10–12. See also Clegg, H. A., Fox, Alan and Thompson,
A. F., *A History of British Trade Unions since 1889*, Vol. 1 (Oxford,
Clarendon Press, 1964), Chaps, 10, 11, 12.

The Pankhurst initiative in 1903 in Manchester owed something to the new assertiveness visible among Lancashire mill girls. They and their thousands of fellow women workers might be appealed to as women by feminists—but they might respond more as workers. The net result could still be the same—men and parties might concede the parliamentary vote not out of a concern for justice between the sexes, but as a recognition of economic necessity and latent political force. What chance was there anyway of any concessions in the immediate future?

Concerned in the nineteenth century to secure the vote for unmarried, but qualified, widows and spinsters the Suffrage movement had, by the early twentieth century, gained it for married and unmarried women—but only in local government, so it was pressing for the parliamentary vote. In the process it had had to recruit among men and women who were neutral to or against its ambitions. Socialists and Radicals in Europe generally, and certainly in England, could be divided on the principle at stake but were adamant against any extension of the propertied vote and cool, if not hostile, to Suffrage organizations. To most Suffragists political opportunity seemed to be at hand, and the knowledge heightened tensions in their movement. What was this opportunity and what were the likely pitfalls lying before any attempt to exploit it?

III. Politics to 1905

. . . the undisguised partisanship of the
Lords . . . cannot continue . . .
W. E. Gladstone, March 1894.

. . . it will be no part of the policy of the
new Liberal Government to introduce a Home
Rule Bill in the next Parliament . . .
H. H. Asquith, October 1905.

The Liberals reaped after 1905 whirlwinds sown in many winds by many hands, not least those of earlier Liberals. The Suffrage whirlwind became a peculiarly intolerable bane of ministerial lives and Mrs. Pankhurst and her daughter Christabel the detested symbols of ministerial frustration. Here was conflict between people who saw themselves, at first at least, as being within the same political fold but found themselves deeply divided on principle. Each group was adamant that the tactics used by the other were, at the personal level, appalling and, at the political level, disastrously illiberal. Both sides acted from not only their political principles, but also their convictions about the lessons to be learnt from the past. In both cases, memories were relatively long, and convictions were not only deeply held but were daily being reinforced after 1906.

It may well be that the origin of Mrs. Pankhurst's behaviour, and ministerial reaction, after 1905 must be sought, in the first place, in events over twenty years earlier. In the general election of 1885 the young Mrs. Pankhurst saw her husband Dr. Richard Pankhurst stand for Rotherhithe as an Independent—and saw him heavily defeated. The principal reason seemed to be that he had failed to gain the Irish vote which, on Parnell's orders, swung against the Liberals for their failure to end coercion in Ireland and grant Home Rule. Emmeline Pankhurst '. . . inveighed against the Irish, but he refused to take umbrage declaring Parnell's policy to be politically sound'.[1] Such composure was to Dr. Pankhurst's credit. It is clear that his wife rarely achieved such detachment and, more significantly, never forgot the lesson she thought she saw in the débâcle. Twenty years later she was citing Parnell as the originator of the policy of *total* opposition to a government in power for reasons of a particular policy. Like Parnell she believed that, on first-class questions in the British system of government, a governing party must either adopt or seek to emasculate 'causes' not particularly its own. A governing party which would not adopt a cause must be coerced either into doing so or coerced sufficiently to allow a bipartisan solution.

Mrs. Pankhurst had her memories but so, too, did Liberal ministers after 1905. They remembered all too well the consequences for the Liberal party of Parnell's policy. Their memories —first and second hand—concerned the fact that Gladstone's conversion to Home Rule in 1886 had split the Liberal party, emasculated the Liberal ministry after 1892, and generally exacerbated existing disagreements among Liberals over other questions of policy. Ministers were only too conscious that the Irish question continued to be divisive. Indeed, they felt they had only just emerged from a period of acute sensitivity on the question.

To understand this sensitivity it is necessary to see these ministers against the backcloth of the preceding ten years in opposition. The questions of Ireland, Empire, and social reform which had divided Liberals in office after 1892 divided them even more deeply after they left office in 1895. The Liberal leader was Lord Rosebery, who had been chosen by Queen Victoria in preference to the 'natural successor'[2] Sir William Harcourt.

[1] Pankhurst, Sylvia, *Life of Emmeline Pankhurst* (T. Werner Laurie, London, 1935), p. 21.

[2] Ensor, R. C. K., *England 1870–1914* (Oxford History of England, 14 vols., Oxford U.P.) (Vol. 14, 1936), p. 215.

Rosebery's position was thus not strong to begin with and his views on Empire weakened it steadily. In October 1896, after W. E. Gladstone (from retirement) had challenged his inaction on the Armenian massacres in Turkey, Rosebery resigned and Harcourt took over as Liberal leader in the Commons. The strains within the party, however, were considerable and, in late 1898, Harcourt resigned leaving the leadership of the Liberals to a choice between H. H. Asquith, who had been Home Secretary in the 1892 Government, and Henry Campbell-Bannerman, who had been Secretary for War. In the event, Asquith declined the offer made by the Whips and Campbell-Bannerman followed Harcourt to a leadership he was to retain for nearly ten years, the last three as Prime Minister.

The changes in the Liberal party leadership were some index of the ferment within Liberalism as a larger movement. The changes in the economy and British society which were providing large numbers of women who *might* be mobilized for Woman Suffrage were, of course, providing increasing numbers of men who might see that enfranchisement as part of a larger liberation, political, social and economic. The Liberal party in the 90s, and through to 1914, was a prime recipient of the tensions generated by considerable societal pressures and a flux of ideas. Major studies of the period are now available which give ample evidence of the context in which the Woman Suffrage impasse after 1906 must be seen.[3] The fact was that the enfranchising of women was seen as a peripheral question by most Radicals both of the older Gladstonian school and, equally, those of the 'newer' men coming into the Liberal party after 1895. This was even more true among most of the men who, after 1900, could hope for office if the party were to win the next election. It followed, therefore, that to mobilize the *potential* following of the Woman Suffrage issue was not easy and to translate this, given the party context, into either a Conservative or Liberal *policy* was a formidable task.

[3] See Emy, H. V., *Liberals, Radicals and Social Politics 1892–1914* (Cambridge U.P., 1973), Mathew, H. G. C., *The Liberal Imperialists. The ideas and politics of a post-Gladstonian élite* (Oxford U.P., 1973).

To appreciate this in the situation after 1906 we need to look more deeply at the Liberal party which provided the government. The first point to note is that the trends visible in the Commons after the 1870s continued. The Liberal party had steadily shed its landed interests before 1900. After 1900 the slow drift away of its commercial and manufacturing interests, visible by the 90s, continued so that by 1910 the number of 'business' Liberals constituted only a third of the parliamentary party.[4] Within this changed situation there was the further consideration that after 1906 it was clear the 'business' element itself was changing. Going slowly were the established 'magnates'—the large, provincial businessmen—to be replaced by the representatives of 'new' business and their professional and journalistic employees and associates. The rapid turnover of Liberal M.P.s after 1895 highlighted these changes. The huge majority of 1906 meant that 205 of the 399 Liberals were 'new' M.P.s. A further 100 had been in Parliament less than ten years.[5] The Liberal party in Parliament after 1906 was in many ways a party of relative newcomers, if not a new party.

In electoral terms, the Liberal party in England was compelled to try to erode Conservative control in Lancashire, Cheshire and London, whilst not weakening itself in the east Midlands, Yorkshire and the north-east. Increasingly after 1900 this double task called for an *entente* with nascent 'Labour' candidates. After this *entente* was established in 1904, between Herbert Gladstone and Ramsay MacDonald, the gains were in fact soon apparent. Despite the losses in 1910, the elections of 1906 and 1910 marked the process of transfer of 33 seats in Lancashire and Cheshire, 21 in London, and 13 in Yorkshire to the Liberal-Labour camp.[6] Between 1885 and 1910 Liberals had increased by 3 per cent their share of the vote in predominantly middle-class constitu-

[4] Emy, H. V., *op. cit.*, p. 101.

[5] *Ibid.*, see pp. 94–103 for a discussion of the changing Liberal Parliamentary Party.

[6] Clarke, P. F., *Lancashire and the New Liberalism* (Cambridge U.P., 1971), pp. 7–14, 398–402.

encies (40 per cent or over) and by nearly 10 per cent in over-whelmingly working-class constituencies (90 per cent or over).

The pact with Labour was the product of Liberal organiza-tional weakness and shortage of funds. The split of 1886 had cost the Liberals such contributors as Derby, Northbrook, Selborne and Hartington. In the 1890s, when the party was under pressure to adopt lower-middle and working-class candidates who would need considerable financial support, it was at a low ebb financi-ally. Evidence of this was the number of seats Liberals failed to contest. In 1895 this had been 112, but by 1900 it was up to 145.[7] Herbert Gladstone became Chief Whip in 1899 but, despite his efforts, as late as May 1902 some 250 seats were without candi-dates.[8] This was the background to the launching of the National Liberal Campaign Fund in 1903 and the pact with Labour in 1904. The structure of the party organization did not help Gladstone. The National Liberal Federation had, locally, to rely on unpaid voluntary Secretaries whose financial support was essential, but whose views often made them unwelcome to Radicals and who in return viewed Radical or Labour candidacies with alarm and disdain.[9] Despite this, however, the pact was con-cluded and in 1906 the Liberals and their allies failed to contest only five seats.

The *entente* with Labour was received in many quarters as, at best, a mixed blessing. It was not, in Dr. Emy's words, seen 'as part of any longer term readjustment of Liberal Labour aspira-tions'.[10] The reasons for this are embedded in the dialogue which was being conducted within the party between the various heirs of Gladstone. This was not a new dialogue but after 1900 the Boer War gave it new life and a new potential for dividing the party. On one side stood the 'new' Radicals whose emphasis was on 'social politics' and the right of the state to intervene in the market economy to alleviate poverty, unemployment, and to re-distribute wealth. On another side stood the more traditional Radicals, based principally in Scotland and Wales, who demanded

[7] Emy, H. V., *op. cit.*, p. 85.
[9] Emy, H. V., *op. cit.*, p. 73.
[8] Emy, H. V., *op. cit.*, p. 93.
[10] Emy, H. V., *op. cit.*, p. 91.

not only such measures as Welsh Church Disestablishment and Home Rule for Ireland, but also more general devolution of power, temperance legislation and taxation of mining royalties and land values.

Another group were the Liberal Imperialists. Their world view is of particular importance because, in the person of H. H. Asquith, they were to provide the Prime Minister who presided over most of the Liberal years in office after 1906. They were much more than simply followers of Rosebery, though they were popularly taken to be so. They feared that the Liberal party was tending to become irrelevant to ever-larger numbers of voters, particularly in England. They hungered to lead what to them seemed the 'centre' vote—the mass of the Labour vote plus a minority of the middle- and upper-class vote. To secure this vote they had to contend with those Liberals whose views made them blind to the danger the Liberal party stood in and to the opportunities that could be seized. These Liberals were the 'faddists' of the National Liberal Federation who wished to democratize the party, and the Celtic fringe who drowned it in a flood of 'contentious marginalia'.[11] Again, there were the Little Englanders who gave the party a pro-Boer, unpatriotic image and finally the 'Tory' Liberals who yearned for 'congealed Gladstonianism', and made a distinctive contribution to the irrelevance of the party.[12]

The 'centre' voter, Liberal Imperialists felt, had little interest in, and could not identify with, these groups. He must be appealed to in ways which he could see as relevant to himself. Hence on foreign affairs the Liberal Imperialists' slogan was 'sane imperialism', while on the domestic front they accepted and developed those ideas implicit in the slogan 'national efficiency'—a rationalization and modernization of political, commercial, educational and military affairs. The Liberal Imperialists opposed the sectionalism of the Labour movement, though were in favour of working-class M.P.s and offered sympathy, if not full support, for the Trades Unions after the Taff Vale decision. On Home Rule for Ireland they were for the 'step by step' approach which was less

[11] Mathew, H. G. C., *op. cit.*, p. 135.   [12] *Ibid.*, p. 135.

contentious, might be got through the Lords, and did not divide the party. They were, as Dr. Mathew describes them, reasonable men who wished to meet at the reasonable centre of politics and decide national as opposed to sectional questions.[13] Their views on what constituted national questions were, by the standards of the 'new' Radicals, very traditional and it was these men, along with the older Radicals, who were to determine Liberal orthodoxy after 1906 and not the Liberal Imperialists. Franchise reform was an exception to this. The Liberal Imperialists doubted whether it would benefit Liberals.[14] Other groups in the party were in favour of a change to a residential franchise qualification but much more divided on Woman Suffrage, and this division helped Asquith personally to have a decisive influence.

Liberals, in their internal debates, reflected the hopes of electoral victory generated by several factors. One of these, the pact with Labour, has already been mentioned. The idea of separate Labour representation was, of course, not new. After 1892 Keir Hardie had sat for three years as an Independent Labour Party (ILP) member and the ILP had kept the aspiration alive after his defeat in 1895. In February 1900 it joined with the Trades Union Congress to launch the Labour Representation Committee. This was to be backed by union funds and would aim for a parliamentary group having its own Whips, which would co-operate with the major parties 'in the direct interest of Labour'. Two candidates only were returned in the Khaki Election of the same year, but the impetus of the Taff Vale ruling of 1901 was more than compensation for the slow start. Within one year Labour Representation Committee membership doubled. In 1902 Liberals in Clitheroe stood aside while David Shackleton took the seat for Labour. In 1903 Will Crooks captured the Tory stronghold of Woolwich, and Arthur Henderson won the first three-cornered contest at Barnard Castle. Balfour's shelving of the Taff Vale issue by the appointment of a Royal Commission, served only to increase union determination to prepare for the election

[13] *Ibid.*, p. 292.   [14] *Ibid.*, p. 134.

that could not long be delayed. Seen from Labour's viewpoint the *entente* with the Liberals was not unattractive. Spared from three-cornered contests, and with Liberal co-operation, Labour could conceivably win up to forty seats.

How such a Labour group would react to the enfranchisement of women was not entirely clear. In Europe socialist thinking was divided on the question. The Anarchist parties were strongly opposed, while the followers of Marx in the Second International, though sympathetic, were adamant in refusing to accept any partial enfranchisement of women and scorned the 'bourgeois' Woman Suffrage movements. The debate continued through to the Stuttgart Conference of 1907, when a part of the British delegation stood out for the acceptance of limited enfranchise-ment as a step toward Adult Suffrage. The general view of the British Labour movement, however, was much more akin to that adopted at the Stuttgart Conference. Limited enfranchisement in Britain meant an extension of the propertied vote. The existence of the plural vote increased the distaste for such an extension since it was assumed that all who could would give wives and daughters sufficient property independently to qualify them, thus increasing the conscious property vote even more.

If Labour was divided so, too, were the Irish. Their attitudes were chiefly conditioned on Suffrage, as on other questions, by its relationship to the question of Irish self-government. The Woman Suffrage issue brought up the whole series of questions related to general franchise reform and on these the Irish were cautious. To understand why this was so it is necessary to examine an important cause of the Parnellite sweep of Ireland in 1885, the Franchise Act of the previous year. The application of the household franchise to the towns and counties had been partly responsible for Parnell's success since, for the first time, the exten-sion applied equally to Ireland. Further, the weakening of the plural member system marked the beginning of the demise of the English Whigs, thus weakening resistance to Gladstone's conver-sion of his party to Home Rule. The Lords had tried to delay the bill by bogging it down in the subject of redistribution of seats.

The eventual solution saw 79 towns of less than 50,000 population lose one of their two members, while the universities and boroughs between 50,000 and 165,000 alone remained two-member constituencies. The rest of the country was cut into single-member constituencies; numerical equality, enshrined in the slogan 'one vote, one value', becoming the governing consideration. Not, however, in Ireland—Gladstone saw to that—and this was one of the Irish factors in the later Woman Suffrage impasse.

Prior to the 1884 Act numerical equality had been a Liberal sentiment, if not a slogan. After the Act the cry 'one vote, one value' became a Tory response whenever the subject of franchise reform was mentioned for, when compared to the remainder of Britain, Ireland was over-represented. In 1801, the number of seats in the Commons granted to Ireland had meant that it was under-represented, a fact Gladstone noted when he asserted that the promise by the Act of Union of not less than 100 seats stood in perpetuity. The questions of numerical equality and redistribution of seats were obvious issues for the Lords to seize on in any new dispute over Home Rule. Ireland's protected status, and its delivery to Parnell by the Act of 1884, had then the potential to involve questions of franchise reform and the redistribution of seats in the Irish problem. In the future, if the Irish Nationalists were to be asked to support franchise reform, their enthusiasm for extra votes for their cause could be offset by the fear that such reform might involve them in a loss of seats in the Commons. Woman Suffrage was to suffer from this fear.

Finally, and very importantly, there were the Tories who, first under Lord Salisbury, and then under A. J. Balfour had been in office since 1895. It was, after all, they who in the period after 1900 helped unite Liberals, restore Labour's momentum and give new hope to the Irish. Against the divisions among Liberals engendered by the Boer War must be set the unifying forces generated by the Education Act of 1902 and the Licensing Act of 1904. Even more heartening to Liberals was the fact that, after May 1903, the government and parliamentary party was splitting over the tariff question raised by the Colonial Secretary Joseph

Chamberlain. Four months after the first speech on the question by Chamberlain, Balfour accepted his resignation and those of the committed Free Traders.[15] For two years thereafter the Tories vainly sought consensus on the question.

The boost to Liberal hopes was considerable. The Education Act, which had rallied most Liberals, had a curious irony for women. By aiming to establish a modern system of education under the aegis of the newly established organs of local government, Balfour had unwittingly emphasized the political impotence of women. On the local government register but unable to sit on local government bodies, women must watch education—a subject agreed to touch their interests—pass out of their direct influence and into the hands of the very bodies which were replacing the School Board system in which they had been active for thirty-two years. A pamphlet of the Women's Liberal Federation of July 1903 claimed that only fifteen of the 110 County and County Borough Councils had appointed women to their Education committees. It did not fail to go on—harking back to the 1888 County Council Act—'We must note, too, that in each case it has been a Conservative Government that has deprived us of our right or failed to protect it. Thus, judging by their consistent action in the past, we cannot fail to imagine that it is the intention of official and reactionary Conservatives to make a clean sweep of women from all public life.'[16]

The Women's Liberal Federation was not alone in sensing the lack of interest of the government. Three months after the Federation statement, Mrs. Pankhurst in Manchester had founded the Women's Social and Political Union. The Union was aimed from the first at Lancashire mill girls who were finding their feet in the world of organized labour. The word 'Social' was put in its title to offer some incentive to middle-class women. Mrs. Pankhurst since the 1890s had moved steadily into Radical and Socialist circles. In 1898 her husband, a friend of C. P. Scott,

[15] Lord Balfour of Burleigh and the Duke of Devonshire resigned.
[16] Pamphlet, Mrs. Bamford Slack, *The Conservative Party and Women Suffrage* (Women's Liberal Federation, July 1903).

had died and, for financial reasons and with Union support, she had accepted the Registrarship of Births and Deaths at Chorlton in Manchester. In 1900, under the auspices of the Independent Labour Party, she had been elected to the Manchester School Board and, one of the lucky few, on its dissolution in March 1903 had been co-opted on to the Manchester Education Committee. She had been horrified, as both Registrar and Guardian, by her contacts with the poor and unemployed. As a member of the Committee on Technical Instruction she noticed that women were excluded from training for many jobs in which their presence was thought to lower wages. The women she invited to her home in October 1903 when the Union was formed were members of the Independent Labour Party. Through the winter of 1903–4 Mrs. Pankhurst and her daughters, Christabel and Sylvia, held their meetings in the Manchester area. The friendship of Keir Hardie proved useful. His influence at the Easter 1904 Cardiff Conference of the Independent Labour Party was sufficient to secure endorsement of Dr. Pankhurst's Woman Suffrage Bill and, too, to have Mrs. Pankhurst elected to the National Administrative Council. In March 1904 the Commons had carried by a majority of 114 a resolution to the effect, 'That the disabilities of women in respect of the Parliamentary franchise ought to be removed by legislation.' The academic nature of this vote, however, was only too clearly revealed fourteen months later when the Commons laughed out a Suffrage Bill introduced by Mr. Bamford Slack, a prominent Liberal. Mrs. Pankhurst, who was present, held an immediate protest meeting outside the House; and her daughter Christabel considered this the real beginning of militancy. Five months were to pass, however, before the national press noticed the new organization.[17]

Mrs. Pankhurst's anger at the Commons action must be seen against the background of frustration elsewhere. In January 1905, at the Labour party conference, her hopes that the conference would follow the lead of the ILP and endorse her bill were dashed. The conference had been asked to endorse 'the Women's

[17] Pankhurst, Sylvia, *op. cit.*, p. 32.

Enfranchisement Bill introduced into Parliament last session, believing it to be an important step toward adult suffrage'. Instead the conference had carried by 483 to 270 a resolution crushing in its finality of tone. 'That this Conference, believing that any Women's Enfranchisement Bill which seeks merely to abolish sex disqualifications would increase the political power of the propertied classes by enfranchising upper and middle class women and leaving the great majority of working women still voteless, hereby expresses its conviction that Adult Suffrage—male and female—is the only Franchise Reform which merits any support from the Labour Members of Parliament.'[18] This resolution it was to affirm by a larger majority at the Belfast conference two years later.

The prestige of Hardie, which had enabled the ILP to swallow endorsing a limited extension bill, could not prevent the Labour party from decisively rejecting it. Writing to Philip Snowden, who had helped defeat her, Mrs. Pankhurst revealed her attitude to the securing of the vote, 'If you knew how I long to get this vote question settled, so that women may get into real social work. I am so weary of it and the long years of struggle, first against ridicule and contempt, and now of indifference and apathy.'[19] Her daughter Christabel was both less weary and less enamoured of the possibilities of success via the Labour party. The Liberals, she sensed, were on the eve of power—they and they alone could grant the vote in the foreseeable future. They must be forced to do so and, if persuasion failed, then coercion must be applied. Conservative indifference, Liberal ambivalence and in 1905 seeming rejection by Labour—the elements of the post 1906 situation were falling into place. The Suffrage movement had numbers and an organizational capacity—and the Liberals must touch on the franchise question when returned to office. Above all, there was in the wings a group of Suffragists who were ready and bitter enough to risk both their reputations and health to try to force a government measure of Suffrage.

[18] Snowden, Philip, *An Autobiography of Philip, Viscount Snowden* (Ivor Nicholson and Watson Ltd., London, 1934), p. 281.   [19] *Ibid.*, p. 283.

Perhaps the final piece, however, was contributed by the Balfour government. If a Liberal government could be forced to produce a government bill then such a measure would mean, almost certainly, that some Irish votes might be required to counter any unsympathetic members of the party. The gaining of these votes was made more difficult by Mr. Gerald Balfour at the Local Government Board. In February 1905 the King's Speech gave notice that there would be legislation on the subject of redistribution—a topic which by precedent was put near the end of the life of Parliament so as to precede an election. In June, Charles Geake of the Liberal Publications Department forwarded a memorandum to the Chief Whip Herbert Gladstone. The burden of it was to point out that if the government could correctly time their redistribution legislation, they might leave it too late for a new register to be compiled. They might, in short, fight the election with redistribution—and on the old register. Suspicion of this was heightened when, in early July, Gerald Balfour gave notice not of a bill but of a resolution—a known tactic of delay. To Liberals this policy was a threat to their election prospects. They were themselves contemplating quite extensive measures of electoral reform: but they were not contemplating taking seats from Ireland as Balfour seemed about to do.

If Liberals were alarmed the Irish were many times more so. With a Liberal government nearing office and the prospect of some form of Home Rule being revived, their numbers—and hence their power to force any government—looked like being reduced by as much as twenty seats. The papers of John Redmond contain a list of amendments he had prepared should a bill come up. One of these proposed a formal renunciation of the Act of Union itself. The one, however, which would have been the centre of the Irish effort proposed raising the minimum number of electors necessary for an M.P. from Balfour's 18,500 to 21,500. If the Unionists asserted that up to twenty seats must be redistributed then this would provide seventeen English seats and Ireland could be left alone. Redmond's own view of any bill was that it would be less a franchise bill than a blow at the Irish. His notes

35

for his speech read '. . . this is not a Reform Bill. It leaves untouched the worst anomalies in representation of people in Great Britain. It creates new anomalies. It does not touch gross injustice whereby . . . [there is] . . . a plurality of votes of [the] wealthy. Not a Reform Bill for England. It is a new Penal Law for Ireland.'[20]

Herbert Paul in an article of August 1905 in *The Nineteenth Century* covered the whole subject thoroughly.[21] The Unionist proposals, he felt, were a means of delaying dissolution, which would have to wait until the new registers were completed. Both parties, he went on, were interested in weakening the Irish, and the Liberals were as anxious for reform as for redistribution. They were in fact torn between the desire to supervise the bill themselves, and the fear of the harsh decisions that that might involve. Such decisions were best left for Unionists, except if taking them helped them avoid their coming defeat. Motives were inevitably very mixed on both sides and, in the event, the decision was never made. In early December Balfour resigned, leaving this and other problems to his successors.

Irish political nerves had been set on edge. With the growing disparity between English and Irish population, their position might not be sustained indefinitely. In October John Morley demanded that Home Rule be in the forefront of a Liberal programme while Rosebery, who opposed this, demanded that Campbell-Bannerman declare himself. Writing to Gladstone in late October, Asquith at least was very clear on his position. 'If we are to get a real majority in the next House of Commons, it can only be by making it perfectly clear to the electors that . . . it will be no part of the policy of the new Liberal Government to introduce a Home Rule Bill in the next Parliament . . . no one intends to devote either the second or third, or any, session to framing and carrying a Bill which will be at once chucked out by

[20] Papers of John Redmond, Folder 'Redistribution 1905'. Irish Nat. Lib. Mss. 15,245.
[21] Paul, Herbert, 'The Representation of Ireland', *The Nineteenth Century*, Vol. 58, No. 342, August 1905, pp. 335–44.

the House of Lords, and will wreck the fortunes of the party for another twenty years.'[22] The Liberals should not risk their chances when Redmond had accepted a 'step by step' approach. With a large majority they could overawe the Lords on many issues, but not on Home Rule which would be the gauntlet inviting conflict. Yet the Irish vote in Britain had to be secured. At the end of November, after Campbell-Bannerman's speech at Stirling, Herbert Gladstone was advising no further commitments other than those agreed to by Asquith. Gladstone's oblique advice was that 'G[rey] and A[squith] now are both on the right side and it is of enormous importance to keep them there. The advanced HR's and Radicals are of course all right, and entirely with you whatever turn you give to HR utterances either to or from it. But the vote which will make or mar our majority is composed of Un[ionist] Free Traders and Educationalists, and anti or weak HR Liberals.'[23] Liberals should, in effect, buy the Irish but at the lowest possible price. In fact no commitment was made—the Irish helped the Liberals more in hope than expectancy.

Just six weeks prior to these letters Grey, at the Manchester Free Trade Hall, had seen Christabel Pankhurst and Annie Kenney hustled out of the meeting when, having previously refused to see a delegation, he then refused to comment on Liberal intentions on Suffrage. When the commotion had subsided he remarked, as though by way of apology, 'That is a question which I could not deal with here tonight because it is not, and I do not think it is likely to be, a Party question.'[24]

Woman Suffrage was on the eve of what might be termed its sensational period. Beginning as an opinion of the *avant-garde* of the nineteenth century, it had fed on and been spread by the legal and educational emancipation of women after 1850, and by

[22] Papers of Herbert, Viscount Gladstone, B.M. Add. Mss. 45989, F. 131–2 Asquith to Gladstone, 22 October 1905.

[23] *Ibid.*, Add. Mss. 45988, F. 205–6, Gladstone to Campbell-Bannerman, 30 November 1905.

[24] Pankhurst, Sylvia, *op. cit.*, p. 52.

1905 was, in the hands of the Pankhursts, to burst on the national consciousness. Its passage was to be burdened by a fateful tie with the whole question of electoral reform and this, by 1905, was itself entangled by ties with the Irish question. The Liberals had many commitments and one of these was electoral reform, particularly an end to the plural voter and a simplified registration process. The Unionists had raised, and would raise, the cry of Irish redistribution in any such event, and they controlled the Lords. The Labour Representation Committee hoped for more M.P.s and was set against any extension of the property vote which would hinder their appearance. The Irish hoped that time was on their side so far as Home Rule was concerned—they also hoped that Liberals would be forced to curb the Lords.

As the election approached it was clear that Woman Suffrage would not be an issue and was unlikely to be mentioned. A majority of Liberal M.P.s and candidates were pledged to it in principle, but there was no agreement on a suitable bill. Some Liberals feared too little and others too much enfranchisement. The Conservatives had a minority who favoured the enfranchisement of separately qualified women. The Labour movement was committeed to opposing any such enfranchisement. With no unanimity in the Liberal leadership there seemed to be deadlock on the question and no chance of progress in the coming Parliament.

Mrs. Pankhurst and her daughters were already resolved to break this deadlock. If the Tories were returned, the Pankhursts were ready to demand that limited enfranchisement toyed with by Disraeli and Salisbury. If the Liberals took office and objected to enfranchising women householders, then the Pankhursts were ready to try to force them to enfranchise those plus married women qualifying on their husbands' qualifications. Neither result could be achieved, they felt, by the polite methods of the older Suffragists. Tea parties would not do it—sensational publicity and martyrdom might. The Press would not be able to resist publishing sensational exploits. If rough treatment of women were involved in these sensations then the pressure on M.P.s and ministers would mount rapidly and break the party political deadlock.

This chapter has examined the long- and short-term political background to the militant explosion of 1905. We must now turn to a detailed examination of the consequences of militancy. The focal point must now be moved from the hustings to the cabinet room, for women would not be enfranchised without the cabinet deciding to support a bill, or agreeing to differ upon it. The problem at first, as will be seen, was to get the cabinet to do anything at all.

IV. Opening Shots

*People always swear at you before they swear
by you.
W. T. Stead to Mrs. Pankhurst, 1905.*

*Well, to tell you the truth, your cause is
not in the swim.
A. J. Balfour to Mrs. Pankhurst, 1905.*

The Liberals under Campbell-Bannerman took office in early
December 1905, and on 12 January 1906 went to the country.
The resulting eighty-four majority over all other parties combined
seemed a decisive rejection of the Unionists—Liberals could be
forgiven for seeing it as a mandate for their programme. Gladstone's ghost must have rested content at such a victory but, in
more than one respect, that ghost was to haunt his party. The
majority was great enough to free Liberals from dependence on
the Irish, but the 'Irish Question' nagged some Liberal con-
sciences and the Nationalists were disciplined and 83 strong.
Labour M.P.s numbered 53, of whom only 29 accepted the Whip
of the Labour Representation Committee—yet their very presence
was 'the sensation of the moment'.[1] Of the 157 Unionists, only
32 were known Balfourites—Chamberlain's triumph could not be
too far away.

Women Suffrage had not been, even remotely, an issue in the
election. In January 1906 it was no more a minor talking point
among ministers. There is no evidence that any serious debate
took place within the larger circle of members of the government.

[1] Ensor, R. C. K., *England 1870–11* (Oxford History of England, in
14 vols., Oxford U.P.), Vol. 14, 1952, p. 386.

No doubt the positions of various members were well known to each other. Asquith, the new Chancellor of the Exchequer, and Lord Loreburn, the new Lord Chancellor, were opposed in principle as was, it may be noted, King Edward. Among the younger men Churchill, McKenna and Herbert Samuel were generally hostile, and Lewis Harcourt very much so. On the other hand the Prime Minister, Grey, Haldane, Herbert Gladstone, Morley, Burns and Lloyd George were sympathetic in a very general fashion. None of them had thought very seriously about it, and the notion of the government promptly bringing in a bill of its own to enfranchise women would have seemed unreal to them. A majority of their party were privately pledged to Woman Suffrage in principle but, as with cabinet members, few had given serious political consideration to the question as it stood in 1906. In the Commons after the election a small group of Liberals promptly formed under Sir Charles Maclaren to consider the implications of Suffrage and to press for a bill.

Despite the growing number of 'new' Radicals in the party, the fact was that the election had been won in traditional Liberal areas and on traditional Liberal issues—Education, Licensing, Free Trade and so on. Herbert Gladstone thought that the party was dominated by 'centre Liberals' flanked to their left by a group of Radicals and Liberal Labour M.P.s whose number Dilke thought could reach fifty.[2] Expectations were high in many quarters. The large Dissenting element in the party—170 M.P.s —was expecting legislation to amend the Balfour Education Act of 1902, and to curb the 'Drink Trade'. In Wales agitation was growing for Church Disestablishment. The Labour M.P.s were hoping for a legislative restoration of the status quo prior to the Taff Vale ruling. Finally, despite the landslide victory, the Liberals were expecting to rationalize the whole matter of franchise qualifications and registration. In particular, there was pressure for an immediate end to the plural voter as a useful beginning to the task of electoral reform. The King's Speech gave

[2] Emy, H. V., *Liberals, Radicals and Social Politics 1892–1914* (Cambridge U.P., 1973), p. 142.

notice of legislation on education, plural voting, Irish cottagers and London rates. It seemed plenty to be going on with.

Getting on with it, however, was the problem from the out-set: before 1906 was out many Liberals had decided that the Lords had resolved to set aside the election victory. The whole of the Liberal tenure of office was to be conditioned by the struggle to curb the Lords, and by the after-effects of that curb. One of the issues that was particularly affected was the Suffrage issue. If the question was involved with electoral reform and if that, in turn, was bound up with redistribution of seats and hence with the Irish problem, as was suggested earlier, then until the Lords were curbed the prospects for Suffrage were bleak indeed. If the Lords were ready to block any measure which reformed the fran-chise for men, then women were very far from gaining the parlia-mentary franchise at all.

Mrs. Pankhurst and her Women's Social and Political Union had thrown down the gauntlet in October 1905. Four months later, when the new Parliament opened, her organization was in exis-tence in London and rapidly gaining support. The opening of Parliament was greeted with a parade. Dilke's hardy annual—his Adult Suffrage Bill—was debated in the light of Woman Suffrage and, in late April, the talking out of Keir Hardie's Suffrage motion produced the first demonstration inside the precincts of the Commons. On 19 May, the Prime Minister met a Suffrage delegation. Confessing himself a convert, he nevertheless promised nothing. Ironically for a future occasion, too, he refused to consider incorporating Suffrage into the Plural Voting Bill then pending for as he said ' . . . the rules of Parliament would not allow it . . . and it would tend to mix up the two reforms'.[3] To the detriment of Plural Voting, he might have added.

Plural Voting, long in the Liberal programme, was one of the main casualties of 1906 so far as the Liberals were concerned. Aware that an extension of the franchise touched the subject of

---

[3] *The Liberal Magazine* (The Liberal Pub. Co., London, 1906), Vol. 14, No. 153, June 1906, p. 299.

redistribution; believing firmly that the plural voter was mostly Unionist—and potent—the government in this bill sought to avoid the former and destroy the latter. Introduced after the summer, the bill soon came under a barrage of Unionist amendments. At the Report Stage in late November, Lord Robert Cecil moved that the Act should come into force the day after the next election or, if before, only on the day that Woman Suffrage came into force—a less than subtle ruse to tempt Suffrage sympathizers into opposing a government measure. The amendment was defeated, as were others of like subtlety, and the bill went to the Lords. There, its life was brief indeed. Despite its disfranchising as opposed to enfranchising nature, the Lords dispatched the bill, claiming that any franchise change was bound —by 1884 precedent—to be accompanied by a redistribution bill.

This destruction of an important piece of Liberal legislation, however specious the precedent, revealed the Liberal dilemma. The Tories in the Lords, it was clear, were being as deliberately obstructive over this as they were over Birrell's Education Bill— also emasculated—but, and this was of importance, they had *some* justice on their side. For Liberals to cry 'One Man, One Vote' for England where—electoral districts being more equal— each vote had somewhat equal value, was one thing. To raise the cry however and treat the over-representation of Ireland as sacrosanct was quite another. The skeletons rattled by Balfour a year previously stirred restlessly. The Lords would oppose an extension of the franchise in the direction sought by Liberals, and Irish over-representation would serve as a not entirely implausible cover.

While the political difficulties inherent in franchise and other questions were becoming apparent at Westminster, some militant Suffragists had earned a new name—Suffragettes—by being imprisoned for trying to force an interview with the Chancellor of the Exchequer, Asquith. In 1906 he was capable of being embarrassed by the event and wrote to Herbert Gladstone, the Home Secretary, that 'I should be delighted if you could see your way clear to mitigate or annul the sentence of the magistrates.'[4] This concern soon gave way to displeasure, and Gladstone was not asked again.

A bitter struggle of wills was thereafter set in motion. One jail sentence merely led to another as the Pankhursts led their growing cohorts into a spiralling sequence of desperation. The Liberals, distrusted by Suffragists since Gladstone's day became, on the Suffrage issue, badly entangled. The Countess of Aberdeen, President of the Women's Liberal Federation which had declared for Suffrage, could write to the Prime Minister of the '... feelings of intense personal mortification'[5] she had on the subject of militancy. But Mrs. Fawcett of the National Union of Women's Suffrage Societies, a prominent Liberal and to the end no believer in militancy, had to admit that the Pankhursts had done more for Suffrage in twelve months than her organization had in as many years. The Labour Party conference of 1906 was again the scene of uproar over the renewed Pankhurst attempt, led by Keir Hardie, to commit it to accepting a limited extension of the franchise to women. Only by a narrow majority, however, did it decide to resist ' . . . any suggested measure to extend the franchise on a property qualification'.[6] In March 1906, there had been a formal call for a Women's Labour League and, when this was actually established on 21 June, there was a brisk fight over the attempt of Mrs. Pethick-Lawrence to aim the League at mere 'removal of sex disability'.[7] The struggle inside the Labour movement was not an unfair reflection of that inside the Liberal party as the first year in office closed.

The year 1907 was for Liberals a somewhat distressing repeat

[4] Papers of Herbert Viscount Gladstone, B.M. Add. Mss. 45989, F. 146, Asquith to Gladstone, 22 June 1906.

[5] Papers of Sir Henry Campbell-Bannerman, B.M., Add. Mss. 41210, F. 49, The Countess of Aberdeen to Campbell-Bannerman, 5 January 1906.

[6] Hamilton, Mary, *Arthur Henderson* (William Heinemann, London, 1938), p. 38.

[7] Papers of the Labour Representation Committee 1900–12. *The Infancy of the Labour Party*, Vol. 2, F. 32.

performance. Disagreement among themselves, and murmurs among the Lords, forced the withdrawal of two attempts at settling the education question. The whole issue of land—tenancy and values—was much in the air, four bills being passed in all. The Lords rendered those on England and Ireland valueless, and destroyed the two concerning Scotland. Campbell-Bannerman's considered reply to these tactics was to secure from the Commons a resolution aiming to limit Lords action on its bills so as to ensure that within the life of a single Parliament 'the final decision of the Commons should prevail'.[8] It was hardly revolutionary and it was all that the Prime Minister was to do. The Lords had been given due warning and, seemingly, they were to elect to ignore it.

Among Campbell-Bannerman's papers, and dating from this time, are notes for a speech on Electoral Reform. They reveal something of the effects of the franchise laws, the significance of the plural voter and Liberal determination to change the situation. 'There are about 600,000 electors in London of whom from $\frac{1}{5}$ to $\frac{1}{6}$ are probably disfranchised on account of the registration and residential qualifications alone [noted the Prime Minister] ... While the poor man is handicapped at every point in the registration system, the property voter—the burgher —is made to count for anything from one vote up to a dozen.'[9]

For Radicals little could be done, unless the Lords were curbed. For Suffragists nothing was done by the government about Suffrage, except to imprison fifty-six Suffragettes after the demonstration which followed the King's Speech. Some were still in prison when, in March, W. H. Dickinson, a prominent London Liberal, introduced his bill to enfranchise unmarried women householders. The debate on this was academic, a purely formal delineation of well-known views, and the bill was talked out. Campbell-Bannerman repeated that the government would give it no time and he personally, he said, could not approve of a bill which

[8] Ensor, R. C. K., *op. cit.*, p. 394.
[9] Campbell-Bannerman Papers, B.M., Add. Mss. 41243 B, F. 240–41.

'. . . will enfranchise a small minority of well to do single women
. . . but will not touch, to any such degree as is necessary, the
mass of working women and working men's wives'. The dilemma
is well put by Dr. Clarke—'The WSPU could only see the pro-
spective new voters in terms of their sex, the Government only
in terms of their class'.[10] Woman Suffrage was impossible anyway
for the moment but, if it could be passed, Liberals were not going
to give votes to the Unionists. In this year two small bills were
enacted: a Qualification of Women Act was passed enabling
women to sit on borough and county councils, and the Deceased
Wife's Sister Act corrected a long-felt anomaly in English marriage law.

Both whetted Suffragist appetites, though militants had much
more to think of. The Pankhurst army had split. Ostensibly, this
was caused by the Pankhurst's refusal to share control of the
Union in any respect—to refuse, as Christabel Pankhurst put it,
to let the army vote on its commander ' . . . in the midst of a
battle'.[11] The decisive arguments were, probably, not about
whether an 'army' was needed but rather about which way it
should march. An alliance with Labour had never pleased
Christabel and when the 1907 Conference rejected anything but
Adult Suffrage—despite Hardie's threatened resignation—she, at
least, was satisfied that the parting of the ways had come. Writing
to Arthur Balfour to invite his party's support she gave her reasons
for this parting: 'The working-class vote is now largely controlled
and organised by Labour politicians and T.U. officials. These
men are very ready to propose restrictions on working women's
labour. There are some who advocate the entire exclusion of
women, whether married or single, from certain industries. There
are those who also desire to close wage earning occupations to
married women.'[12] Believing thus, she saw Adult Suffrage only

[10] Clarke, P. F., *Lancashire and the New Liberalism* (Cambridge U.P.,
1971), p. 121.

[11] Pankhurst, Christabel, *Unshackled. The Story of How We Won The
Vote* (Hutchinson, London, 1959), p. 82.

[12] Papers of A. J. Balfour, B.M. Add. Mss. 49793, F. 35, Christabel
Pankhurst to Balfour, 28 October 1907.

as a trap for Woman Suffrage and one from which in due course would emerge the real goal of such men, namely universal *male* suffrage and an anti-feminist majority. No wonder Christabel saw the seceders as 'renegades who plotted to sell the movement to the Labour Party'.[13]

The logic of being a feminist before all else was fairly simple. Extensions of the franchise in England had had a recent history of 'instalment plans' with demands for total enfranchisement being regarded as visionary or revolutionary. It followed, there-fore, that a party which refused to ask only for a first instalment was, in effect, refusing all. When such a party was in any case visibly shot through with doubts on the principle at stake, then the logic seemed even more inescapable. Enemies might sneer all they cared that the provincial Pankhursts had been dazzled by London's Tory drawing-rooms. Nevertheless the case was per-suasive. The Labour party was no vehicle for Christabel and Emm-eline Pankhurst and, in effect, they broke with it.

The effects of the break were many and potent. The Pank-hursts, and especially Christabel, were now poised to be masters of an increasingly desperate Suffrage situation. The motto of the WSPU was changed from 'We demand the Parliamentary Vote for women on the same terms as it may be granted to men' to 'Tax paying women are entitled to the Parliamentary Vote' and this symbolized more than a change of tone. The split had constituted a backhanded invitation to Balfour to enact in due course what Disraeli and Salisbury had considered, namely, the giving of the vote to separately qualified women. This confirmed the Labour movement in its conviction that, if possible, no such thing must be allowed. Equally it persuaded Liberals that the Pankhursts were a Tory battering ram aimed not at the party in power, as much as at the *Liberal* party in power. A stiffening of attitudes all round was inevitable. Ironically in the Tory party any front bench sympathy was more than offset by back bench fury at militancy.

[13] See Billington-Greig, T., *The Militant Suffrage Movement* (Frank Palmer, London, 1912), p. 84.

A symbol of the new Commons position was not long in coming. In April 1908, on Campbell-Bannerman's retirement, Asquith became Prime Minister. A convinced and determined opponent of Suffrage was now in charge of the government. Here was no Grey or Haldane with a record of private sympathy—albeit verbal—for Suffrage. Here was no Lloyd George capable of being pressured by the attractions of an exploitable cause. Campbell-Bannerman had nicknamed Asquith the 'sledgehammer' for his force in debate, and it was an apt name for a man capable of rotund Latinesque syntax and rhetoric at a moment's notice on whatever part of whichever bill he was summoned to defend or attack. Here was a man who had climbed the 'greasy pole' of political success and was entering into what he and his friends regarded as his legitimate inheritance.

Asquith treasured fond memories of his apolitical first wife, and thrust on by Margot Tennent's consuming passion—influence and importance by position and ability, not votes—he was no admirer of those he faced on the Suffrage question. Indeed, quite the reverse. For years he treasured the opinion that, while militants were criminals, the non-militants were lacking in soundness of judgement in their unnatural demands. Democracy, he argued, had no quarrel with distinctions based on sex. If, however, most women wished for the vote and could show that Parliament neglected their interests then, and only then, would Suffrage become practical politics.

He succeeded at a time when the party pressures on the government were considerable. Steadily since 1906 Radicals had pressed ministers into facing the problems of unemployment and poverty, into considering further legislation for pensions, an 'eight hours' bill for miners and a bill to assist the provision of working-class housing. The struggle over the naval estimates in 1907 was part of a larger ministerial struggle over the need for more direct taxation for social reforms. By the spring of 1908 a Miners bill and a bill for pensions had been given priority and the nettle of increasing taxes had been grasped.[14]

[14] Emy, H. V., *op. cit.*, pp. 169–75.

On Woman Suffrage, however, there was no equivalent readiness to move—at least at first. In January Asquith saw a delegation of the National Union led by the wily and knowledge-able Mrs. Fawcett. He was quite blunt; the government would not introduce a measure of its own, nor would it offer facilities for a Private Member's bill. He was as good as his word. In late February the Second Reading of Mr. Stanger's bill, yet another limited enfranchisement proposal, received a curt refusal of facil-ities. The Home Secretary, Gladstone, who was a Suffragist, de-clared in the debate that, while Suffragists had won the political argument, '. . . the time comes when political dynamics are far more important than political arguments'.[15] To the militants this was justification of their conduct but, ironically, Gladstone was undoubtedly reflecting on the fact that political dynamics were operating against Suffrage, and that militancy was strengthening the trend. The bill received a majority of 179 after what was purely a formal debate. Gladstone, earlier in the month, had received Royal congratulations on his handling of militancy. The Home Secretary, however, revealed his sympathies clearly when, prior to the first big Albert Hall meeting of the Pankhursts, he released Mrs. Pankhurst and her associates and coolly informed the King 'Mr. Gladstone considered it was desirable to give Mrs. Pankhurst and her five associates the benefit of one day's remis-sion, so that they could take part in a large and legitimate demon-stration.'[16]

In May, Asquith saw a delegation of sixty Liberal M.P.s led by Stanger, who requested further time for his bill. However, the Prime Minister declared any such promise of time to be '. . . out of the question'; although he did make the significant admission that the government must bring in a scheme of elec-toral reform, and that this should be so framed as to allow a Suffrage amendment initiated by the Commons. His colleagues were divided, he explained, but two-thirds of them were for this procedure.

[15] Parliamentary Reports, 4th Series, Vol. 185, Col. 242.
[16] Gladstone Papers, *ibid.*, F. 71, Gladstone to Lord Knollys, 21 March 1908.

Given that the front benches could not agree sufficiently on the principle or implementation of Suffrage for women this seemed, at first glance, to be a reasonably promising solution to the embarrassing question. The government would not, as a government, resist an amendment to its bill giving women the vote if this was the clear majority opinion of the House of Commons. The growth of the militant wing of the movement and the relative decline of the older NUWSS would be halted, perhaps reversed. The embarrassing, indeed infuriating, spectacles in Parliament Square, the sight of police manhandling demonstrating women, rich and poor alike, the fear of what the more desperate spirits might soon attempt—all might be halted and turned to the channels of persuasion. It was, after all, common knowledge that a majority of M.P.s were for Woman Suffrage.

Were they, however, for it in the context of a contentious Reform Bill? The Liberals had a minority adamantly opposed to any Suffrage measure and the sixty to eighty Tories strongly in favour were therefore crucial. Would they stay faithful despite the Whips in what could become a bitter party battle? Equally, when the government's existence was put into the balance, would many Liberals not waver in face of party pressures, and what would happen if the Whips went on? In a situation in which Suffrage introduced varying degrees of uncertainty into the calculations of party managers inside Parliament, and even greater degrees of uncertainty into electoral behaviour in the country, it was certain that other changes in the franchise would be preferred in both parties, and certainly among the Irish Nationalists if they were to be asked.

What seemed therefore a not unreasonable offer at first glance did not stand up well to close inspection in the light of the realities of party conflict. The more women the proposed amendment enfranchised, the more Tories would melt away; the less, the more Liberal and Labour M.P.s would waver. True, as Bertrand Russell noted to Mrs. Fawcett, it was the first time a Prime Minister had offered anything to Suffrage. It was equally true that what might *seem* a useful way to divert the Suffrage cause might boomerang. In a House weary of the issue, the government might find itself unable to sabotage and hence have to carry Suffrage or lose its bill. But, nevertheless, as the WSPU promptly publicized, the 'offer' evaded the question of whether the government would carry through something they could not, as a government, bring in and to which a third of the cabinet was deeply opposed. Was it simply a delaying tactic to gain time for the force to go out of the campaign? Were not such suspicions heightened when, six days after the meeting with Stanger, Asquith, in reply to a parliamentary question, adamantly denied that it was the government's intention to introduce a franchise bill containing a grant of Woman Suffrage? His tone revealed very clearly that a majority vote in the Commons would not convert him on the question. Mr. Asquith was not open to persuasion for the moment.

V. Ministerial Dilemmas

If we are to keep the whole thing constitutional among thousands of women we must have some help.
Lady Frances Balfour, November 1908.

. . . our machinery is not adapted for the immediate and successful treatment of questions on which parties are divided . . .
Herbert Gladstone, September 1909.

Woman Suffrage had not been on the Liberal agenda in 1906 and by late 1908 it was, at very best, a question to be dealt with when, and if, the government could get a comprehensive franchise bill through both Houses. That, in itself, would be a near miracle, given that the Tory leadership in the Lords seemed bent on emasculating Liberal legislation. For many Liberals it had became crystal clear that, to survive, the government must bring these intentions of the Lords into an unmistakable and electorally profitable focus. Licensing, Land, Education—none of these would serve as the best *casus belli*—through the Lords' rejection of the Licensing Bill on Second Reading in October 1908 had, usefully, provoked Royal wrath and some Tory misgivings. The Budget was, however, in preparation under the wily Lloyd George—now that was a different matter. As December came in preparations were in hand for the possibility that the Tories would be foolish enough to tamper even with the Budget.

Suffrage was not a possibility until larger questions had been settled. The message was clearly delivered at the Albert Hall on 5 December by the man most directly involved in these larger questions, Lloyd George. Speaking to the Women's Liberal Federation just after Asquith had, in the Commons, again denied that the government was contemplating a Reform Bill, the Chancellor of the Exchequer left little unsaid. Suffrage, he asserted, had neither major party committed to it. A majority of the Liberal cabinet and party were for it, but in both parties there were hostile minorities, '. . . of influential, responsible men whom no party would risk a quarrel with . . . I will tell you why. Both parties have suffered so severely from great splits . . . that they are not very anxious to embark on any enterprise which involves that.' The Prime Minister's declaration, he went on, meant that Suffrage would be a question when the Reform Bill was introduced. This could not be immediately for—'. . . it is a recognized condition of political legislation that you must not bring in a suffrage bill unless you are prepared to dissolve the moment the register comes into operation . . . therefore, it is perfectly clear that a bill of that kind will be an indication that the Prime Minister has come to the conclusion that Parliament should go to the country. Well, that is not yet. We have a few accounts to settle before then.'[1] Answering questions from members of the Federation he denied that a Suffrage clause imposed by the Commons was an invitation to the Lords to reject the bill. He denied, too, that the government were hoping for rejection of any such bill so as to go to the country on that issue. He repeated that a franchise bill would need to be timed to enable the government to dissolve after a new register had been drawn up. It was an impressive performance though something of an optimistic assessment of the Suffrage situation. Lloyd George was fighting a holding action not for the sake of Suffrage so much as for the Liberal party in the country. Dissension was spreading and inaction on Suffrage was only one cause of it. It was vital to persuade the Women's Liberal Federation that the government had a strategy and was not drifting in frustrated impotence on to the rocks at the next election.

Militant protest was rising in several sectors of British society,

[1] Pamphlet, *Lloyd George on Women's Suffrage at the Albert Hall, December 5, 1909.* (Women's Liberal Federation, London, 1910.)

notably in the world of the Labour movement. Edwardian England was rife with protest at poverty, bad housing and social inequalities of many kinds. After 1908 real wages declined slowly but steadily and the 'condition of the people' was fertile ground for the spread of French Syndicalist notions of direct action and militant protest. Mrs. Pankhurst took as her model for the marches of Suffragettes, the marches of the unemployed and poor being organized in Poplar by George Lansbury. Christabel's conviction that a rotten, male-dominated society would yield only to startling shocks to its security and sensibilities was derived in part from the example of the Russian anarchist *émigrés* in England whom she met after the abortive Russian revolution of 1905.

Suffragists, generally, were very far from seeking to emulate such people, believing that such methods were not needed in 'democratic' England. Yet they needed evidence for hope and there seemed precious little. Well placed to see what was happening was Lady Frances Balfour, the wife of Gerald Balfour and a prominent leader in the NUWSS. A friend of Asquith since the 1890s, she quoted with some asperity in her autobiography the conviction of a later colleague of Asquith's that he 'had only one sincere conviction and that was his antagonism to the vote being given to women'.[2] In 1908 she was clearly very worried over spreading militancy. Writing to Mrs. Fawcett in November— that is, before the Lloyd George speech—on the proposed merger with the dissident Pankhurst followers, now formed into the Women's Franchise League, she noted how they had defended militancy 'because they were losing both members and money because they did nothing . . . The desertions . . . were all in favour of the SPU [Pankhursts]. This tallies very much with the dissension in our own society.'[3] The same day in two letters to her friend the Home Secretary she apprised him of the would-be merger and the dangerous situation developing among Suffra-

[2] Balfour, Lady F., *Ne Obliviscaris* (Hodder and Stoughton, London, 1930), p. 158.
[3] Papers of Mrs. M. G. Fawcett, Vol. 2, Lady F. Balfour to Mrs. Fawcett, 6 November 1908.

gists. 'Asquith always thinks he can have a day to day, hand to mouth policy in this matter. Every time it is put off, the strength of the movement grows. If we are to keep the whole thing constitutional among thousands of women we must have some help.'[4] Five days later, reporting to Mrs. Fawcett on her conversation with the Home Secretary, she related his view that the militants —'. . . are finding it difficult to get people to go to prison, and he thinks the Government are crushing the movement . . . Asquith, he told me, was quite uninterested . . . I saw he felt he could not answer for Asquith. I also saw he thought that the constitutionalists should be encouraged . . . In truth, he knows he has no influence in the Cabinet . . . There is no doubt just how militantism has hurt us.'[5]

Lady Frances was clearly not persuaded of the grounds for Gladstone's optimism over militancy. The frankness of Lloyd George's speech at the Albert Hall was evidence that he, too, was unconvinced that inactivity in the Commons and violence in Parliament Square was good policy. Politicians generally, however, were infuriated by the Pankhursts. Their fury expressed itself in December when Lords and Commons passed Lord Robert Cecil's Public Meetings Bill—designed to control militant activities—in a total of ninety minutes of actual debate.

The Suffrage movement and the cause it embodied had, in the event, to take its chances. To hand was the great justification of governmental inaction. The Lloyd George Budget of 1909 dominated the politics of the year and its consequences those of the following two. A full discussion of its nature and reception by Parliament has no place in this narrative. In so far as it addressed itself to 'the condition of the people' it could be said to have been a reaction to conditions dramatized—among many others—by Suffragists, who argued that the vote would enable women not merely to defend their interests, but also those of their children. Of

[4] Papers of Herbert Viscount Gladstone, B.M. Add. Mss. 46066, F. 105–106, Lady F. Balfour to Gladstone, 6 November 1908.
[5] Fawcett Papers, Vol. 2, Lady F. Balfour to Mrs. Fawcett, 11 November 1908.

much more direct importance to the Suffrage cause was that the Budget was a clear challenge to the Lords and one which the government expected them to take up. Once the battle had begun, it was clear that there could be no franchise bill before an election. Such a bill could only follow a victory over the Lords, or be lost for years in a Liberal débâcle. If Lloyd George had correctly assessed the government's position and if Suffrage was to be allowed only as an accepted amendment to a government bill, that is, if Asquith stood aside, then Suffragists must wait until the government was ready. First deal with the Lords and then other things would follow.

Thus the fierce militancy of the ensuing years, while it kept the Suffrage pot boiling, served little real purpose, losing in Parliament more supporters than were gained, and hardening enemies as little else could have. The so-called Reform Bill, even without Suffrage, was causing some trouble. Lord Crewe, the Liberal leader in the Lords and a confessed opponent of Suffrage, publicly denounced those who thought that the franchise qualifications would be widened for men, and esepcially those who imagined that anything could be done in the present Parliament. Asquith put his position quite clearly in a forthright letter to Gladstone who, at Leeds, had said—so Asquith had heard—that if a Woman Suffrage amendment to a Reform Bill were carried the government would support it. 'What I have said is, that, if such an amendment is moved, the Government as a Government, will not oppose it . . . I further said, or implied, that if such an amendment were carried, the Government would not on that account cease to proceed with their Bill . . . But that is a very different thing from saying that *as a Government* they will thenceforward "heartily support" an addition to their Bill to which I, and several of my colleagues are, and shall remain, "heartily" hostile.'[6] Such sentiments were exactly what he had said publicly—there was no hint here of any duplicity. This exchange was just a few days before the King's Speech which made no mention of Suffrage and hence

[6] Gladstone Papers, B.M. Add. Mss. 45989, F. 216–17, Asquith to Gladstone, 11 February 1909.

led to twenty-six arrests among Suffragists bent on forcing a meeting with Asquith.

So far as the eventual Reform Bill was concerned, anyway, Asquith was only too well aware of the view put succinctly by F. J. Shaw in a current pamphlet: 'As usual Ireland blocks the way. Any adequate final scheme of reform implies an adequate plan of redistribution. But any redistribution bill that is not a farce must greatly reduce the representation of Ireland, and that to a Liberal Government means a Home Rule Bill.'[7] In March, Howard's Adult Suffrage Bill was given a Second Reading by a majority of thirty-four in another formal debate. Two weeks previously W. T. Stead, informed by Gladstone of Asquith's eventual sympathy for Suffrage, replied gloomily 'I hope you are right about Asquith. I have every disposition to think well of him, but whether he can discriminate between bluff and reality remains to be seen.'[8] That capacity was being tested to the full all year long as the fury of the Opposition and the Lords grew. A letter in April to the Scots Liberal Whip, the Master of Elibank, from T. P. O'Connor throws light on one potentially important aspect of the struggle: '. . . the time is fast approaching when we shall be able no longer to resist the trend of our people to vote for the Tory, rather than support a Liberal who, by reducing Home Rule to a pious opinion, practically postpones it to the Greek Kalends. What makes the situation more aggravating is that all this could be transformed by a few simple words from the head of the Government, expressing his determination to make Home Rule one of the issues at the next election.'[9] Those 'simple words' would be hard to drag from Asquith and harder still to embody in legislation.

Outside government circles two interesting developments may be noticed. In late June there met at Caxton Hall the first meeting

[7] Pamphlet, Shaw, F. J., *Women's Votes and Party Tactics* (N.P., 1909).
[8] Gladstone Papers, B.M. Add. Mss. 46066, F. 299, W. T. Stead to Gladstone, 4 March 1909.
[9] Papers of Alexander Murray, Master of Elibank, Folder 1, F. 210–11, T. P. O'Connor to Elibank, 14 April 1909.

E

of the Council of the Women's National Anti-Suffrage League under the chairmanship of Lady Jersey. It was reported that membership was 9,000 and that there existed 95 affiliated branches. Four hundred public meetings had so far been held, it was claimed. With Mrs. Humphry Ward and Lord Curzon as forceful guiding lights the organization did not lack prestige leadership thereafter. Coming as this meeting did in 1909 after the Asquith declaration, and with a general election pending, Suffrage was beginning to enter the realm of political possibility and hence was capable of stirring reaction. Meanwhile, militancy continued. During 1909 Mrs. Pankhurst's followers began to use the hunger strike as a means of escaping prison sentences. This soon resulted in government action. In August, answering a Royal query, Asquith indicated that the cabinet supported the Home Secretary's refusal to give Suffragettes the privileges of First Division treatment in prison, and by September forcible feeding was authorized and begun. By December, the Royal opinion having hardened, Crewe, in place of Asquith, was reporting a cabinet refusal to make severe examples of the offenders.[10]

The Home Secretary was clearly under contradictory pressures from above and below. As a suffragist sympathizer his police function was all the harder to carry out, as his correspondence reveals. In early September he had begun to correspond with Mr. and Mrs. Wilfred Richmond, a Hampstead headmaster and his wife. On 11 September 1909, Mr. Richmond in a letter asked 'Have the statistical calculations as to the numbers of working women who would be enfranchised by the removal of the sex bar under the present franchise law, put the P.M. into a position to modify his attitude as to a really democratic measure etc.? I.e. would he now accept and adopt (if it were passed) an amendment to the Government measure which simply removed the sex bar?'[11] There is no record of a reply to this but, in two subsequent

[10] Papers of the Earl of Oxford and Asquith. Box 5. Cabinet Letters 1908–10, F. 140, Asquith to H.M. the King, 4 August 1909.
[11] Gladstone Papers, *ibid.*, F. 165. W. Richmond to Gladstone, 11 September 1909.

letters, Gladstone laid out the position as he saw it in the light of militancy and cabinet divisions. '. . . our machinery is not adapted for the immediate and successful treatment of questions on which parties are divided . . . I am afraid the outlook is thoroughly bad . . . Assuming a General Election to come early, or following the failure of the Prime Minister's proposal, what will be the position at a General Election? It will be chaotic, because men will not be bullied solely by the action of a few hundred women.' Again, five days later—'The franchise question was not before the country in the Election of 1906 . . . It is . . . obvious that this Government qua Government cannot take up this question . . . No violence that unthinking zealots may attempt can alter solid facts. The murder of Cavendish in 1882 destroyed the chance of Home Rule.'[12] The Home Secretary was clearly very concerned at the possibility of real personal danger to the Prime Minister. But he was also concerned to alleviate the cause of threats to Mr. Asquith. In early October he wrote to a fellow suffragist sympathizer, Grey, the Foreign Secretary. Having, himself, already accepted the offer of the post of Governor-General of South Africa he wrote, as he said, as someone now 'outside the fight'.

The Woman's Suffrage question appears to me to be in a most awkward position if we are to be faced very soon with a General Election. It is curious that it has never been raised in the Cabinet . . . On the merits the Cabinet gives 15 for and 4 against. Perhaps 16 to 3. Roughly, that nearly represents, at any rate, academic opinion on our side in the H. of C. Those of us who are for the vote have not pressed our views, because the question was not before the country in January 1906 . . . but the position is obviously untenable at a General Election. And our responsibility has been made more marked by the P.M.'s concession of the Reform Bill amendment . . . The postion of the P.M. and 2 or 3 of our colleagues is wholly adverse to the suffrage . . . The essential difficulty of the position is the division of the parties on the subject. The usual political machine 'tinplating' won't work. It may be chimerical, but is it impossible to remove the question *wholly* from politics? . . . Unionists and Liberals are equally pestered. Bob Cecil told me he thought their

[12] *Ibid.*, F. 182–3, 202. Gladstone to W. Richmond.

difficulty in office would be greater than ours. Why should not the leaders of the parties agree that the position should be determined by the votes of men returned at the next election, and that whatever Government may be in power, if there is a majority for the vote a Bill should be brought in by the Government before the end of Parliament. Resignations would not be expected . . . the general principle of the Bill . . . which could be agreed . . . would be equal franchise with men.[13]

Grey promptly replied that 'I do not think enough has been made of the [Asquith] pledge, and if some means could be found of making a reasoned statement of the attitude of the Government, pointing out what has been promised and how it has been accepted as reasonable by the bulk of women suffragists and ignored by the minority, it might do good.'[14] Asquith, however, was not to be pushed and there is no record of formal cabinet discussion. On the question of the Budget, however, he had little choice. Writing to Crewe in October of a possible dissolution he noted 'In my judgement . . . the outcome of an election fought under such conditions was not unlikely to be a very small majority either way between the British parties, with the deciding voice in critical matters left to the Irish: a very undesirable state of things.'[15]

Gladstone was not a dominating figure in the cabinet and his initiative led to no cabinet discussion. The issue was not included in the Election and this was not accidental. Crewe in November noted to a deputation of Suffragists that 'If they did make this question a definite issue at the General Election it would undoubtedly involve changes in those men who now held office in the Party.'[16] At the Local Government Board, John Burns was condemning militancy six days later to the activists of the Women's Liberal Federation—'. . . the strongest arguments

[13] *Ibid.*, B.M. Add. Mss. 45992, F. 132–5, Gladstone to Grey, 11 October 1909.

[14] *Ibid.*, F. 136–7. Grey to Gladstone, 15 October 1909.

[15] Asquith Papers, Box 46, Crewe–Asquith Correspondence, F. 182, 6 October 1909.

[16] *Liberal Magazine* (Liberal Pub. Co., London, 1910), Vol. 17, No. 195, December 1909, p. 660.

against Woman Suffrage have been supplied by the perverted aims and mistaken methods of a few irresponsible people'.[17] Mrs. Pankhurst, it seemed, was playing into the hands of her enemies.

On 30 November the Lords rejected the Budget, thus making a January election inevitable and redoubling Suffrage efforts to push Suffrage into the campaign. It seems clear that one of Gladstone's aims was the neutralization of the Suffrage question and particularly of the militants. One person, at least, in high Suffrage circles must have received a letter similar to that sent earlier to Grey. In December, the journalist H. N. Brailsford was replying that he, at least, was for the idea, and that it might work. Gladstone, receiving this, hastened to reply—'I have not made any proposals, either directly or indirectly, on behalf of the Government, nor have I any authority whatever to enter into negotiations with the Women's Social and Political Union.'[18] The same day he wrote to H. W. Massingham urging him to correct Brailsford's misapprehension, 'You will remember that I was careful to say that it was impossible for the Government to negotiate with people who were in open defiance of the law. In fact, of course, if I attempted any such proceeding my colleagues would repudiate my authority.'[19] Ministers, even retiring ministers, could burn their fingers over the Suffrage question. Gladstone hastily drew back from the results of his own initiative—he would not see Brailsford.

That a destruction of the Lords' Veto made Home Rule a strong possibility was clear, but Redmond himself was anything but certain of this and pressed hard for the inclusion of Home Rule in the party platform. Writing to Lord Morley in late November before the Budget rejection, he had threatened to swing the Irish vote to the Tories unless there was 'an official declaration which will show clearly that the Home Rule issue is in-

[17] Papers of John Burns, B.M. Add. Mss. 46301, F. 15, Burns to Marie Corbett.
[18] Gladstone Papers, B.M. Add. Mss. 46068, F. 13–16, Gladstone to H. N. Brailsford, 6 December 1909.
[19] *Ibid.*, Add. Mss. 46042, F. 67–8, Gladstone to H. W. Massingham, 6 December 1909.

volved in the issue of the House of Lords'.[20] Speaking at a Liberal rally at the Albert Hall on 10 December Asquith had little to say on Home Rule, but a fair amount on electoral reform. 'Our franchise law is still encumbered by artificial distinctions. . . . Some of the most crying of them we have in this Parliament attempted to remedy in the Plural Voting and London Election Bills. . . . You know what was their fate and how it was brought about. . . . Nearly two years ago I declared on behalf of the present Government that, in the event which we then contemplated, of our bringing in a Reform Bill, we should make the insertion of a suffragist amendment an open question for the House of Commons to decide. Through no intention, and no fault, of ours that opportunity for raising the matter has been taken away. Our friends and fellow workers of the Women's Liberal Federation have asked me to say that my declaration survives the expiring Parliament . . . and that their cause—so far as the Government is concerned—shall be no worse off in the new Parliament.'[21]

In October 1907 Balfour declared he was for inclusion of Suffrage in a Reform Bill, but carefully made his declaration *not* as Unionist leader. In December 1909 he had sanctioned a pre-election statement which said that 'the policy . . . of granting or withholding the Parliamentary vote to women in existing circumstances is no portion of the official programme of the Unionist Party. Each member of it is at liberty now as he has always been, to hold and to express what view he pleases upon the subject without any derogation from his Party loyalty.' He also wrote to the militant Annie Kenney 'If there is no division of opinion on matters of general policy corresponding to the division between the sexes, an extension of the Suffrage would have no important effect either on legislation or administration.'[22] There was little joy in that quarter for Suffragists.

[20] Papers of John Redmond, Envelope 13, Redmond to John Morley 27 November 1909. Irish Nat. Lib. Mss. 15,207.

[21] Asquith Papers, Box 48, Speeches, 1907–9, F. 160–2.

[22] Papers of A. J. Balfour, B.M. Add. Mss. 49793, F. 59 and F. 123 Balfour to Miss Annie Kenney, 3 January 1910.

Thus the country went to the polls with Suffrage not at issue between the parties and both front benches trying to avoid such a situation. Much bigger questions were at stake. For Liberals, with little to show by way of legislation and much promised, the election was critical. For Balfour, defeat might mean his removal from the leadership. For the Irish Nationalists the curbing of the Lords veto would bring Home Rule much nearer, if not make it a certainty. Which way would the electoral verdict be given?

VI.   The Eye of the Storm

Now we are not quite our own masters.
Lewis Harcourt to Asquith, January 1910.

L. G. clearly does not regard next year as our
effective opportunity.
H. N. Brailsford to Edith How Martyn,
May 1911.

An Edwardian general election was a somewhat leisurely affair
with polling going on for several days and a rather unhurried
count. In January 1910 the election began on the 12th and Liberal seats began toppling fairly steadily to the Tories. By the 24th
Christabel Pankhurst, writing to Lady Betty Balfour about the
Tory government-to-be, could assert that 'there will be less for
the women in this Union to suffer in the new Government. I have
already four promises from Unionist members to ballot for the
Women's Enfranchisement Bill.'[1] Clearly, several Tories, cocka-
hoop over the coming victory, had promised a fairly prompt
limited enfranchisement of women, perhaps of those qualified on
the local government register. The Lords would not oppose a
Tory bill.

Appearances proved deceptive. Despite their gain of 102 Liberal and 13 Labour seats, the Tories were still the minority party
in the Commons and it was Asquith and not Balfour who formed
the new government. It was satisfying to stay at Downing Street
but the party had suffered a political and moral defeat and the
outlook was not good. 'Well,' wrote Harcourt on 26 January,

[1] Balfour, Lady Betty, Ed., *Letters of Constance Lytton* (William
Heinemann, London, 1925), pp. 192–3.

'the elections *are* a disappointment to you and me. I had hoped not to lose more than eighty seats on the ballots. Now we are not quite our own masters. Everything seems to point to an inevitable second Election this summer: but has Pease got (or can get) the funds to fight it? I know that before Christmas the Tories were reckoning on exactly this situation and that they would break up financially.'[2] Asquith shared these concerns and his fears of dependence on the Irish had been proved real enough. That dependence would stimulate the unrest and turmoil already apparent in the country. The Liberals had sought a mandate to curb the Lords. What they returned to was a situation in which the Irish could be portrayed as dominating the government. Only careful political manoeuvre could begin to mitigate such a state— a task made the more difficult since King Edward had refused to guarantee the necessary peers until a second election had taken place. Considerations of franchise reform could only complicate things in the Commons, and the Lords would anyway reject a Liberal bill. For the Liberal government therefore, nothing must impede, and everything must await, the checking of the Lords.

Woman Suffrage moves, then, until August 1911 have a strong air of unreality. Any judgement on the wisdom of the Pankhurst tactics must be made against this background. The leaders must have been aware of Liberal determination to curb the Lords and yet they were to break the truce in 1910 when it was quite clear, in advance, that Asquith would not accept the Conciliation Bill. Militancy had made Woman Suffrage newsworthy and this fact was of real importance, for the non-militants had never been able to rouse general interest among voters. Lloyd George questioned the timing of their policy, but he was too shrewd a politician not to see that even hostile interest could be turned into support more easily than could inertia and apathy. While the Pankhursts, particularly Christabel, may justly be accused of pressing violent protest blindly or for its own sake, this need not totally detract

[2] Papers of the Earl of Oxford and Asquith, Vol. 12, Misc. Corres. 1909–10, F. 77–9 A, Harcourt to Asquith, 26 January 1910.

from the long-term value of a policy which kept the issue constantly in the public mind.

Since the Tories had lost the election, any chance of a government supported bill, giving a limited enfranchisement to women, was non-existent. Needs must then that an attempt be made to find a bipartisan solution minimally acceptable to a majority of the Commons rather than a measure which would enable Asquith to put the Whips on against it. In February 1910, an all-party Conciliation Committee was formed to bring in a bill which Unionists could accept, but yet which did not create proportionately more propertied voters. This initiative was welcomed by virtually all Suffragists. The Pankhursts accepted it and called a truce—a fact welcomed by the cabinet which, nevertheless, continued to see the Conciliation Committee largely as a Tory initiative. The bill produced by the Committee promised the vote to Women Occupiers and Householders. It confirmed the status of Suffrage as an intractable problem. Tories would not accept the enfranchising of the wives of qualified electors—a step which would add millions of working-class women to the register. In this they had some Liberal support. A larger section of the Liberal party, however, would accept no bill without this addition, and in this had general ministerial support. At the centre of debate stood a Prime Minister personally opposed to the whole business and very clear that no one in his party should be distracted by marginal matters of this kind, when so much else was at stake.

Such was the line Asquith took in early June when Suffrage, for the first recorded time, was discussed in full cabinet. Reporting to the King afterwards Asquith noted 'The Cabinet were of the opinion that no facilities could be afforded to such a Bill [when] . . . the Government have expressed their intention to take no further contentious business of their own.' This was confirmed after further discussion on 15 June, the day after the first reading took place. Finally, on 23 June, the report to the King noted 'It was ultimately decided that towards the close of the session time should be afforded . . . [but] . . . only a guarded statement made as to the future.'[3] As Balfour reported to Christabel Pankhurst a few days later, '. . . the Government is not only divided on the question of Suffrage, but those who are in favour of Suffrage are divided as to the *kind* of measure which they will consent to support'.[4]

To understand the context in which the cabinet was working we must look back to other events inside and outside Parliament, and principally to the Budget proposals and the allied question of a proposed Parliament Act. The spring of 1910 was rife with rumours on both subjects and their consequences. In February, as the Conciliation Committee was being formed, Harcourt was writing to Asquith that if the King refused guarantees of the creation of peers after a second election 'it is Revolution'.[5] The Labour party was gathering for its Conference at Newport, Monmouth. Arthur Henderson attacked the government for its slowness over electoral reform and led the defeat of a resolution urging opposition to any Reform Bill should Suffrage be excluded. His view of Suffrage prospects was revealed in a striking example of prescient comment. Noting that when a Reform Bill came in it would be a government measure, he went on 'Supposing, by an accident, this particular point was left out? Supposing it was moved in the House of Commons that women be included, and that it was defeated? Were the Labour Party to be bound hand and foot to offer uncompromising opposition to the whole Bill because it did not include that one point?'[6] Certainly not, the delegates felt—and voted accordingly. Later that month a letter from the Master of Elibank to Asquith touched on the same subject when it noted that Redmond had, during the Election, urged the Irish to vote Liberal, among other reasons because the

[3] *Ibid.*, Box 5 Cabinet Letters 1908–10, F. 230, Asquith to H.M. the King, 23 June 1910.

[4] Papers of A. J. Balfour, B.M. Add. Mss. 49793, F. 92–3, Balfour to C. Pankhurst, 27 June 1909.

[5] Asquith Papers, Misc. Corres. 1909–10, F. 114–15, Harcourt to Asquith, 7 February 1910.

[6] Report of Tenth Annual Conference of the Labour Party, Newport, 9–11 February 1910, p. 75.

Unionists had threatened redistribution for Ireland. Redmond had tied himself too closely to the Liberals for threats of crossing the floor to be taken seriously—though, as was seen, these were made as the Irish pressed for the Veto Resolution. The Irish now had their opportunity—the curbing of the Lords would certainly open the way for electoral reform which included redistribution, but only after they ceased to have cause to be concerned and had gained their Home Rule Act. Evidence that Liberals *had* to care, Home Rule or no, was given in early March in a report to Asquith on the election results of the Home Counties. Asquith annotated his copy, noting '78 county districts where the ownership vote exceeds Conservative majority'.[7] He would want that corrected when possible.

In mid-April the Commons passed the substance of the future Parliament Act in three Resolutions. The Irish had insisted on this and, having secured it, they then fell in with the Budget proposals which went through on 27 April 1910. The Lords promptly passed them without a division—as Liberals had expected, indeed feared they would do. At this point, the whole scene was changed by the death of Edward on 6 May.

The event postponed for seven months the clash of Houses which was being prepared by the party leaders. At first, the cabinet was unwilling to talk of compromise—the Irish naturally resisted—but eventually agreed to a Constitutional Conference which prolonged the affair until November. As Harcourt noted on 9 May, 'You will find on your return a very strong feeling here that it would be indecent for us to force a Constitutional crisis at this moment upon the new King. Of course, there is no real ground of *reason* in this, because if the Constitution is out of gear, the sooner it is revived the better. But I cannot deny that, politically, we should incur much public odium.'[8] The Conciliation Bill, almost farcically, came in at this time of deceptive calm. It had been given an unopposed First Reading in June. On 11 and 12 of July a full-dress debate took place with anti-

[7] Asquith Papers, Box 48, Folder 2, 1 March 1910.
[8] *Ibid.*, Vol. 12, F. 136–8, Harcourt to Asquith, 9 May 1910.

Suffragists such as F. E. Smith and Asquith attacking the principle and Suffrage supporters such as Lloyd George and Churchill attacking the bill itself. Prior to the debate Lady Selborne, the President of the Conservative and Unionist Woman Suffrage Society, had appealed to Austen Chamberlain to appreciate what was at stake. Noting that Suffrage pressure was rising and that Asquith was increasingly alone in his opposition in cabinet, she appealed to Chamberlain to help 'enlist the naturally Conservative force of property owning women on the Unionist side . . .' With Front Bench help from the Conservative party she asserted 'we might stave off adult suffrage for another generation'.[9] Here was some confirmation of Radical suspicions and further evidence of the intractability of the Suffrage problem. The bill was sent to the limbo of the Committee of the Whole House and the parties returned to their dialogue on the Parliament Act which went on through the summer.

By the autumn, as the crisis approached, a worried Grey was writing to Asquith of the need for a coalition for '. . . Constructive legislation including the settlement of Home Rule . . . If the Conference breaks up without agreement I foresee the break up of the Liberal Party . . . The other party, of course, is paralysed and useless, but behind us there are explosive and useless forces, and I do not believe we can resume the old fight against the Lords by ourselves, without division.'[10] Asquith, outwardly, remained as stolid as ever. Interestingly, at this time, Elibank was drafting a list of topics which covered every conceivable Liberal policy—except any mention of franchise reform, even of plural voting.[11] If, as is likely, the list was an election platform then the franchise issue was again to be left out. Such in the event was the case—the campaign ignored everything save the Lords and Ireland.

Asquith announced the end of the Conference on 10 November, and the dissolution came a week later. On 9 November a

[9] Papers of Austen Chamberlain AC/8/6/4, Maud, Lady Selborne to Austen Chamberlain, July 1910.
[10] Asquith Papers, *ibid.*, F. 214–15, Grey to Asquith, 26 October 1910.
[11] Papers of Alexander Murray, Master of Elibank, Folder 2A, F. 123–7.

memorandum sent to the Master of Elibank—now the Liberal
Chief Whip—from Jesse Herbert of the Liberal Central Office,
had forecast a gain of twenty-nine seats. In the Conference, proposals for electoral reform clearly had played a part in the deadlock. Asquith, in a letter to Balfour of early November, discussed
the proposals for legislation 'organic' to the constitution which
the Lords could still have delay or veto powers over after passage
of the proposed Parliament Act. He declared '. . . the proposal
now under consideration would include in the same category all
Reform Bills, big or small (including the abolition of plural
voting), all the most modest schemes of devolution, and indeed
practically all measures of *political*, as distinguished from social
and economic change . . . It is here where the shoe pinches so
acutely that the Party would reject it.'[1][2]

At about this time Elibank received an impassioned letter from
Walter MacLaren—'I beg of you, as a loyal supporter, to do
your utmost to avert the impending disaster of driving the
Women's Movement into open hostility . . . even the Women's
Liberal Federation . . . [urges facilities for the modified Conciliation Bill] . . . I urge that the Prime Minister in refusing further
facilities for the Bill this year should pledge the Government that
they will give complete facilities . . . during the next session of
Parliament . . . you cannot afford, on the eve of a General
Election, to drive the whole Woman's Movement into the most
bitter opposition, nor to weaken, and in many cases alienate the
support of the most active Liberal women workers.'[1][3] This fear of
Liberal women workers is of some interest. The Women's Liberal
Federation had sought to ensure that no parliamentary candidate
was adopted who was not sympathetic to Woman Suffrage. Yet
the Federation had to face the fact that, though a majority of
Liberals were in favour, the opposition of Asquith was quite
decisive. With the Pankhursts and the National Union stressing

[12] Balfour Papers, Add. Mss. 49692, F. 108, Asquith to Balfour, 3
November 1910.
[13] Elibank Papers, *ibid.*, Folder 2A F. 131–3, Walter MacLaren to Elibank, 11 November 1910.

the Federation's impotence many of its members must have been tempted, at the very least, to refuse any further work for the party. M.P.s and ministers might publicly minimize the danger; they could not ignore it.

On 18 November the dissolution was formally announced amid unprecedented scenes of violence in Parliament Square. Trying to see M.P.s and ministers—they claimed in legal groups of twelve —followers of the Pankhursts were met with serried and by now unsympathetic ranks of Metropolitan Police. This was 'Black Friday' and its victims entered into the ever-growing pantheon of Suffragette heroes and martyrs. Nothing quite like it had been seen before in the precincts of Parliament. For six long, violent, sometimes brutal, hours there raged in Parliament Square what can only be described as a battle between the police and not the unemployed, the homeless or the destitute of whom there were plenty, but middle- and upper-middle-class women of all ages: the very women, in fact, who could have been mothers, wives or daughters to the M.P.s the police were protecting with such vigour, once they overcame their deference toward 'ladies'. Asquith had left the House and avoided Mrs. Pankhurst at the Stranger's Entrance. As Lord Castlereagh moved that the Conciliation Bill be regarded as government business, and members ever more anxiously pressed for action, he returned and promised to make a statement the following Tuesday. As darkness fell the total of arrests reached nearly 120, many being in need of medical treatment. The following day all were released, Churchill the Home Secretary declaring in a statement that 'no public advantage' would be gained by prosecution.

On the Tuesday in the promised statement there was no mention of the Conciliation Bill as such, and no promise of time for anything but a 'democratic' bill and that not, by inference, in the first session. The Pankhurst answer was the spirited attempt made on the following day to beard Asquith in No. 10. In consequence there occurred what the papers dubbed the 'Battle of Downing Street'. Asquith had to be rescued by the police and hustled away in a taxi, while the level of violence quickly matched that of the previous Friday. Some 185 arrests were made, two of the arrested being seriously injured. Coming so soon after 'Black Friday' the battle deepened the impression of a government getting into ever more turbulent political waters, and of a society in which passions on all sides were rising rapidly. The spectacle of middle- and upper-class politicians hiding from their women folk was hardly good for national self-confidence.

The election campaign was conducted amidst the guerrilla war of Suffragette interjections and the increasingly desperate, if peaceful, attempts of non-militants, particularly Liberals, to get the cabinet to change course. The result was further loss of two Liberal seats, thus making the two major parties equal at 272 seats and highlighting the seemingly total dependence of the Liberals on the Irish and Labour parties, each of whom had gained two seats.

For five years the cabinet had fended off Woman Suffrage. At first the argument had been that there was no demonstrated demand from women and the question had not been at issue in 1906. Then it had been argued that Suffrage was unwise and inexpedient—the militants were proof of this unwisdom, should any be needed. Finally the theme had been that token enfranchisement was a Tory measure and the Lords would allow no other. By January of 1911 as Parliament met, all these arguments rang ever more hollow and the last, in particular, seemed on the eve of its destruction.

One prominent and well-placed observer, at least, thought the election victory was sufficient reason for believing that the Liberals would finally act. Speaking to the Pankhurst organization in early January 1911, H. N. Brailsford clearly exuded confidence. 'Mr. B. seems to think that the Government really now intend to enfranchise women; that they have a new spell of power, and a majority to enable them to pass a more "Democratic" measure . . . [this] . . . has changed the situation. During last year their hand was stayed because, expecting an election immediately, they were determined not to create a million votes for the Tory Party as they genuinely believe the Conciliation Bill would do. They also expected to be returned to power with a majority sufficient to enable them to carry a Woman Suffrage Bill of their own making. Both these considerations are now altered. A five years' retention of power [is] expected as the only means of carrying their Home Rule Bill: a fourth victory at a General Election [was] not to be counted upon, women's votes or no women's votes: with their present majority, [it would be] impossible to carry through the Houses a Woman's Bill exceeding the limits of what all parties would jointly sanction.'[14] In other words the election had stymied a government bill—the Liberals must concede some kind of all-party solution. One way or another, however, there would be action. The Labour party, in conference at Leicester a month later, concerned itself with this prospect. It reaffirmed its opposition to a limited enfranchisement, Mr Russell of the Cab Drivers noting that the Conciliation Bill '. . . intensified the inequalities that existed, and would have added to the power of the propertied classes by adding a large number of plural votes'.[15] Hardie's reply that the existing sex disqualification hindered the arrival of Adult Suffrage had no effect on the delegates. The party executive was positively instructed to bring in Adult Suffrage bills whenever possible, and the Conference was the scene of many indirect attacks on the Parliamentary party for its subservience to Liberal necessities and sensitivities. Labour, at least, would be wary of any all-party settlement.

The government, meanwhile, prepared to bring in the Parliament Bill as soon as possible. If it had any thoughts of franchise reform, they were almost certainly concerned with the plural voter. On 11 January, a letter to Gladstone from Charles Geake of the Liberal Publications Department noted, 'The plural voter lost us at least 40 seats this time, thanks to the smallness of the majorities.'[16] A month later, one day after the Parliament Act

[14] Papers of Mrs. Pankhurst, Folder 'Demonstrations and Political Action'.
[15] Report of the Eleventh Annual Conference of the Labour Party, Leicester, 1–3 February 1911, p. 102.
[16] Gladstone Papers, *ibid*., F. 199, Geake to Gladstone, 11 January 1911.

F

had been reintroduced, Asquith was reporting to the King that the day's cabinet had been 'mainly concerned with the abuses of plural voting'. It had been decided to take no action until certain reports were in, and various ideas had been drafted as bills. This was reaffirmed at a cabinet meeting a month later.

Meanwhile, the Conciliation Bill was reintroduced. Speaking in March to the Conservative and Unionist Women's Franchise Association, Lord Selborne attacked the opposition of Lloyd George to the bill and declared that 'We know the real reason. The real reason is that there has been a matter of calculation. If the calculation had shown the majority of those million women were likely to vote Radical, we should have heard nothing about an undemocratic Bill. Their attitude is simply due to the fact that the calculation was to the effect that the majority would probably vote Unionist.'[17] This was hardly news to the Suffragists he faced, and no consolation. C. P. Scott, the Editor of the *Manchester Guardian*, later recorded a conversation he had had with Haldane. Scott had asked him to speak for Suffrage in Manchester. Haldane refused, but replied—'. . . the present position of the question to which both sides in the Cabinet had frankly agreed was more favourable than we could well have expected —he referred, of course, to Asquith's promise of Government time for all stages of the Bill within the lifetime of the present Parliament—that of late the feeling in the Cabinet had become distinctly less favourable . . . I pointed out that the life of Parliament was precarious, and asked how soon we might look for a fulfilment of the pledge. He said that of course it ought not to be long delayed and that they were pressing this point in Cabinet.'[18] There was no indication here of any fresh thinking on the subject. The coal strike, then in progress, no doubt drove all franchise considerations out of the heads of ministers. Yet it could be argued, and Suffragists did argue, that franchise reform would go toward

[17] Pamphlet *Earl of Selborne's Address at the Hotel Cecil Mar. 9, 1911* (Conservative and Unionist Women's Franchise Assoc., 1911).

[18] Hammond, J. L., *C. P. Scott* (G. Bell and Son Ltd., London, 1934), p. 104.

helping ameliorate 'the social condition of the people', the urgent need for which the Northern Liberal Federation, then in conference, recognized. Widespread industrial unrest, Suffragists argued, was a symptom of social decay that demanded radical solutions from the Liberal government and, while these would be chiefly social and economic in content, there was need of some political reform. The curbing of the hereditary chamber was necessary but so, too, was electoral reform including a broadening of the franchise. A government, they felt, forced by great unrest into radical policies *might* be the government which was capable of solving the political deadlock over Woman Suffrage.

In the first week of May, as the Parliament Act completed its Committee Stage in the House, and two days before the new Conciliation Bill was to be given its first Reading, Asquith reported to the King that 'In regard to the Woman Suffrage Bill, which comes up on Friday, it was agreed that Ministers should use their discretion both in speaking and voting. The Prime Minister is paired against the Bill, and Mr. Balfour for it.'[19] The bill, as amended in Committee, appeared without the £10 householder qualification, and claimed to give the vote to all genuine women householders, a million in number. It was given its Third Reading by a majority of 167, and referred to the limbo of the Committee of the Whole House. Writing three days later to his sister-in-law, Balfour noted 'the immediate difficulties, both in the House and out of it, seem to me much greater than they suppose, and not only this Government, but any other Government which may succeed it, must find themselves face to face with a problem which I will not say is insoluble, but which is, unquestionably, very hard of solution'.[20]

The difficulty was only too apparent in the cabinet, which discussed the issue in mid-May. Asquith reported to the King that 'Sir E. Grey, Mr. Runciman, Mr. Birrell, and Lord Haldane were in favour of, at any rate, giving the House an opportunity of deciding by vote whether it desired to proceed further with

[19] Asquith Papers, Vol. 6, F. 32, Asquith to H.M. the King, 3 May 1911.
[20] Balfour, Lady Betty, *Ed.*, *op. cit.*, pp. 219–20.

the Bill this year. The Lord Chancellor, the Chancellor of the Exchequer, and Mr. McKenna were opposed to this course, as were apparently a majority of the Cabinet. The Chief Whip was instructed to survey the ground and the final decision, at the Prime Minister's suggestion, was postponed until next week.'[24] That decision was indeed taken a week later—one day after the Parliament Act reached the Lords—and Asquith reported that '. . . in view of the prospects of business [the Cabinet would] . . . refuse it any further facilities this Session, but . . . [undertook] . . . to give it a week for its consideration . . . in the next Session'.[22] Of this last meeting, John Burns clearly felt that Grey was the Suffrage leader in the cabinet. His diary has the note that one of the 'important issues [was] W S by G'.[23] H. N. Brailsford put down the decision reached to Lloyd George's credit. 'L. G. clearly does not regard next year as our effective opportunity. That is to come later, if ever. This is only another academic occasion thrown in to keep silly women quiet. Two days in 1910. Five days in 1912.'[24]

Nothing useful had been promised. While Suffragists considered their courses of action, all eyes turned to the Lords as they considered the Parliament Act. Through June and July the bill, in Committee Stage, was amended. By 20 July, on the Third Reading, a substantial 'No Surrender' movement had arisen under Lords Willoughby de Broke and Halsbury. Though Lansdowne and Balfour had been told of the King's pledge to create peers—on 18 July—the situation drifted dangerously until Curzon organized an opposition movement. Once this gathered momentum, friends of Diehards in the Commons might howl down the Prime Minister but they could not prevent the curbing of the Lords. Many years of Liberal frustrations seemed to roll away when on 10 August, in a 97 degree temperature, amidst the

[21] Asquith Papers, *ibid*., F. 38, Asquith to H.M. the King, 17 May 1911.

[22] *Ibid*., F. 39, Asquith to H.M. the King, 24 May 1911.

[23] Papers of John Burns, B.M. Add. Mss. 46333, Diary, 24 May 1911.

[24] Pankhurst Papers, H. N. Brailsford to Edith How Martyn, 25 May 1911.

execrations of the Diehards, the Lords passed the bill by 131 to 114—29: Unionist peers, the archbishops, and 11 of the 13 bishops present providing the majority.

The Parliament Act as passed provided that passage of a measure through three successive Commons' sessions, not necessarily in the same Parliament, meant that it became law despite three rejections by the Lords, so long as two years had elapsed between its introduction and final Third Reading in the Commons. The life of Parliament was cut from seven to five years, while bills designated Money Bills by the Speaker passed, under certain conditions, immediately into effect without the Lords' assent.

If the Lords had been the great obstacle to basic Liberal measures and had prevented the party from seeking an accommodation with the Suffragists then, on the face of things, the way was open now for such an accommodation. The Parliament Act, however, brought into being a certain logic of its own. The Liberal government would wish to go to the electorate with its programme enacted rather than with part of it needing a further submission to Parliament. Again, all experience told against winning a fourth election. Hence, assuming the government to be thinking of an election in late 1914, then the parts of its programme certain to meet Lords' rejection must be introduced first in 1912 to ensure the required three submissions. This created a very real problem with regard to time—a problem the opposition would exploit, and a problem at its height in 1912.

Electoral reform—manhood or woman suffrage—complicated things further. By precedent, the passage of such bills was usually followed by a dissolution once the new register was in being. To put a Reform Bill into the programme was to risk having the hand of the government forced by a Tory inspired passage through the Lords solely to force an election. With major, complex bills such as Home Rule, Welsh Disestablishment, and National Insurance pending, and Suffrage and general electoral reform having no great section of Liberals ardently behind them, then Suffrage as an issue stood to be ignored on grounds of time, danger, and a fear for party unity. It was very clear to knowledgeable Suffragists that, to overcome these obstacles, their cause must be championed at cabinet level, by a minister or ministers of stature sufficient to ensure that the avoiding of the issue would be more dangerous than its solution. The passage of the Parliament Act had opened the door to legislative progress but in the immediate future the prospect for Suffrage was depressing. On the Liberal side a hostile Prime Minister, a divided cabinet and an overloaded schedule. On the Tory side profound bitterness and division over the Parliament Act.[25] The seeming 'acquiescence' of the Balfour-Lansdowne leadership in the actions of the Liberal government made its survival highly dubious and made any chance of a bipartisan solution to Suffrage highly unlikely. A Suffragist surveying the prospect could almost be forgiven for being defeatist.

[25] The bitter divisions in the Tory Party are seen in Gollin, A.M. *The Observer and J. L. Garvin 1908–14* (Oxford U.P., 1960), pp. 332–46.

VII.   The Cabinet and the New Reform Bill

Henry's present position is hopeless and even ridiculous—he alone never saw the importance of enjoining silence on Grey and L. George, and this fearful mistake will break us to a certainty.
Margot Asquith to Elibank, 28 January 1912.

I think we are now nearly out of the wood.
Asquith to Elibank, 30 March 1912.

England sweltered in the hottest summer since 1868. The whole country seemed restless, the rhetorical fury in Parliament reflecting the deep-rooted discontents in Edwardian society. A wave of labour unrest the previous year had culminated in the ominous dispatch of troops to control rioting in the South Wales coalfields at Ton-y-Pandy. Now in 1911 the fever of protest was visibly abroad. In June there had been the seamen's and firemen's strike which ended in the capitulation of the shipping companies. Almost immediately there followed sporadic strikes in the engineering industry. Smouldering throughout July there was the threat of a dock strike and, to complete ministerial preoccupation, the Agadir crisis with Germany brought the country perilously near to war. The defusing of this crisis by Lloyd George's speech at the Mansion House on 21 July did little in the docks or on the railways. On 1 August the ports were paralysed and the ending of this strike, on the day after the Lords passed the Parliament Act, came just in time to enable the government to countermand an order bringing 20,000 troops to the capital. Just five days later England faced its first national rail strike. Troops camped in

London parks and among some observers the conviction grew that revolution might be no longer a French monopoly. The storm which had destroyed the Lords veto might destroy the whole system—social, economic, and political.

Such was the atmosphere in which Suffragists of all kinds agitated and in which ministers and politicians generally had to move. Crisis heightened political passions, educating and changing some minds and driving others deeper into intransigent bitterness and vindictive resolution. The Suffrage cause was inevitably seen from many points of view. In the East End of London, Sylvia Pankhurst was preaching Suffrage as part of the rise of the Labour movement, while in the West End, her sister Christabel was portraying it as strengthening 'constitutionalism'—a cover word in 1911 for the Conservative cause and party. Most Liberals feared and distrusted both causes and the Liberal cabinet mirrored their fears.

The Lords had been conquered, but the conquest had created a political situation that promised no real gain for Suffrage unless it were championed in the cabinet and fought for before the party and the country. In the autumn of 1911 Suffragists had to console themselves with only the promise of parliamentary time in 1912 for the Conciliation Bill. Before the election, the government's objection had been to the limited nature of the bill and, when this had been modified somewhat, the objection was to the lack of time. In 1912, the government was pledged to give a week to the bill and not to interfere if the Commons voted for its passage. This pledge was to force consideration of the issue inside the cabinet in the winter of 1911–12, opponents of the bill joining with opponents of Suffrage to resist it. If the Liberals could not agree on the Conciliation Bill, could they agree on any bill which offered some hope of a way out on Suffrage?

The autumn, then, was alive with expectation inside and outside Parliament. Major pieces of legislation were pending and an extra session of Parliament had been called. The atmosphere is well captured in a letter from the Fabian Clifford Sharp to Sidney and Beatrice Webb, then on a world tour. 'I have gathered from one or two quarters (e.g. Freemantle and Bathurst) that the Tories are still seeing visions of bloody revolution which will inevitably come upon them if they don't behave—and very likely if they do. I think it gives an enormous impetus to "social reform" of all kinds —we ought to see a lot done in the next few years. I gather that Lloyd George is already planning a great measure to dissolve upon, three years hence. He told Gardiner that it would be so revolutionary that even the *Daily News* would fear to follow him! He has got to produce something big in 1913 and 14—and (one) . . . can't deny that he had courage enough for anything. What Gardiner says he is going to deal with is Housing . . . There is a bare possibility that we might force him to take up Poor Law Reform.'[1]

So far as Suffrage was concerned, there were fears involving widening 'wrecking' amendments to the Conciliation Bill when it appeared. Lord Robert Cecil from the Right, and Philip Snowden from the Left warned of this possibility. Snowden, in a pamphlet issued at the time, argued persuasively that three-quarters of the women householders to be given the vote would be working-class, and that there was no support in Parliament for Adult Suffrage. Any attempt, he said, to widen the Conciliation Bill to give the vote to householders and wives of householders would wreck it, since Unionists plus 100 Liberals and 30 Nationalists would reject it. Herbert Samuel writing in September to Herbert Gladstone—now Governor-General of South Africa—revealed one question that was still exercising the government. 'Plural Voting will come on early next year—in good time to pass under the provisions of the Parliament Act and to have effect before the next General Election—at least so we hope. But we may possibly have to face a decline in trade and little to offer but Home Rule and Welsh Disestablishment—and £400 a year paid to M.P.'s!'[2] The assumption here, very clearly, was that the Conciliation Bill

[1] Papers of Beatrice and Sidney Webb, Section 2, Folder 4, E. C. Sharp to Webb 28 July 1911.
[2] Papers of Herbert, Viscount Gladstone, B.M. Add. Mss. 45992, Vol. 8, F. 264. Samuel to Gladstone, 15 September 1911.

would be out of the way, that Suffrage could not possibly be a factor in the next election.

Mr. Samuel, however, was reckoning without the Chancellor of the Exchequer. Lloyd George, it is clear, was working for the demise of the Conciliation Bill; but not, it would seem, for the demise of Suffrage. Plural Voting and a reform of the registration laws—following the 'Latchkey' case of 1905—indeed, the whole subject of electoral reform was on his mind. A week before Samuel was forecasting only Plural Voting legislation, he had written to the Master of Elibank, the Liberal Chief Whip, a letter which set out the Liberal dilemma and deserves full quotation.

I am very concerned about next year's Registration Bill. As you know, I proposed to the Cabinet, having first of all obtained your assent . . . to drop the idea of introducing a mere Plural Voting Bill and to immediately press forward a measure for simplification and extension of the franchise. To this they agreed. Unless it is introduced and sent up to the Lords next year it will not be available for the next General Election. Now, as you know, I am rather keen that you should circularise all your leading agents, with a view to ascertaining from them what the defects of the present system are . . .what the effect would be in their Districts of a simple, residential qualification. In this connection I am very concerned about our pledges on the Female Suffrage question. We seem to be playing straight into the hands of the enemy. The Conciliation Bill would, on balance, add hundreds of thousands of votes throughout the country to the strength of the Tory Party. We would thus lose more than we could possibly gain out of the Registration Bill. We have never really faced the situation manfully and courageously. I think the Liberal Party ought to make up its mind as a whole that it will either have an extended franchise which would put working men's wives on to the Register, as well as spinsters and widows, or that it will have no female franchise at all. The only basis upon which Women's Suffrage has been conceded in any other country, as you know, is the former. Now, it looks to me that . . . we are likely to find ourselves in the position of putting this wretched Conciliation Bill through the House of Commons, sending it to the Lords, and eventually getting it through. Say what you will, that spells disaster to Liberalism; and unless you take it in hand and take it at once, this catastrophe is inevitable.[3]

The issue was put here clearly enough. As H. N. Brailsford was to point out in December in the pamphlet of the National Union of Women's Suffrage Societies, the 'Latchkey' case's redefinition of a householder—a lodger with his own door key could now be one—had forced the government to consider the possibility of gaining this new 'householder vote'. But, as Lloyd George was here noting, any gain from this and from an end of Plural Voting, might be offset by a limited extension of Woman Suffrage. He, at least, realized that piecemeal electoral reform was potentially highly dangerous. In the words of a student of the period 'In obstructing the claim for woman suffrage the Liberal Party risked being hoist with its own petard'.[4]

Whatever Snowden and others might say, the Conciliation Bill smacked of a 'property bill'. If the Liberal party could not face enfranchising women householders *and* wives of householders— the crucial addition—then it must not be forced into acquiescing in its own embarrassment and confusion. There is no record of Elibank's reply to this letter and none, either, of cabinet discussion that was relayed to the King. There also exists no evidence that Suffragists suspected that the government was reviewing the whole electoral issue—Mrs. Pankhurst, for example, was in America on a fund-raising tour. Quite quietly, on 7 November, as if to compete for headlines with Balfour's resignation as Leader of the Opposition, Asquith announced to a deputation of the People's Suffrage Federation that it was a government intention to introduce in the next session a bill which, while virtually giving manhood suffrage, would be capable of being amended by the Commons to include a democratic extension of Suffrage.

The Times declared Asquith's announcement to be 'the explosion of a mine beneath the Conciliation Bill'. Lord Knollys

[3] Papers of Alexander Murray, Master of Elibank, Folder 2B, P. 301–4, Lloyd George to Elibank, 5 September 1911.

[4] Clarke, P. F., *Lancashire and the New Liberalism* (Cambridge U.P., 1969), p. 129.

wrote to the Prime Minister that the King '. . . cannot help feeling surprised that you made no reference to the Manhood Franchise Bill, when you had so good an opportunity on Monday. He thinks you are mistaken in supposing that it was generally known that the Cabinet had decided on such a Bill . . . much less that it was to be introduced next session.'[5] The Women's Social and Political Union, reflecting militant surprise and outrage, declared immediate hostilities. Lady Betty Balfour, writing to Beatrice Webb, noted—'This is his reply to the vigorous five years campaign for a limited Woman S. Bill—when there has not been one meeting throughout the country for an Adult Suffrage Bill, and no one wants an equality which will put women in a majority. He cynically said he would still let us have one week to discuss the Conciliation Bill, queering our pitch, frightening off all Conservative support—and uniting all Adult Suffragists against the Bill.'[6]

On 13 November Asquith told the Commons that a redistribution bill would accompany the Reform Bill and, four days later saw a deputation of Suffragists from the NUWSS, the Pankhurst followers, the Women's Freedom League and the Conservative and Unionist Women's Suffrage Association, all opposed to manhood suffrage before the removal of the sex disqualification. The cautious Mrs. Fawcett of the National Union urged that Suffrage be incorporated into the bill by the government. Asquith, in his reply, declared that the government hoped the bill would pass through all its stages in 1912 and that a Suffrage amendment, if carried, would be regarded as an integral part of the bill.

On the face of things this seemed a reasonable procedure for a cabinet which, though divided on Suffrage, was in earnest about electoral reform. Haldane, at least, was one who thought so. Writing to his sister Elizabeth, an ardent Suffragist, he noted 'As you will have seen, the decision about Woman Suffrage is a very satisfactory one. We have been busy over the matter for some time, and I think the question is in a far more practical

[5] Papers of The Earl of Oxford and Asquith, Box 3, Knollys to Asquith, 8 November 1911.

[6] Webb Papers, Lady Betty Balfour to B. Webb, 10 November 1911.

shape than it ever has been in my time. The prospects are really very good if these tiresome women would only leave things on our assurance.'[7] Suffragists could, perhaps, be forgiven for doubting ministerial assurances—even one so positive from Lloyd George who had told the deputation—'If you find next year as a result of this "trick" that several millions of women have been added in a bill to the franchise, and that this bill has been sent to the House of Lords by the Government, and that the Government stand by this Bill, whatever the Lords do, those who have committed themselves in this ill-conditioned suggestion will look very foolish.'[8]

Nevertheless, there was a prompt revival of militancy on a large scale and this was of no little importance. The first target was the government itself in its Whitehall heartland. Four days after Asquith saw the mixed deputation of Suffragists, Mrs. Pethick-Lawrence led a 'raid' on government buildings which, before it petered out, resulted in broken windows in virtually every ministry, and at the homes of Haldane and John Burns. The assault on property had begun.

Lloyd George and his friends had succeeded in putting the franchise question into the forefront of politics, where it had not been in 1910 and certainly not in 1906. True, Suffrage was not included in the government bill—but it would be accepted by the government if it could be shown to be an issue commanding national support. C. P. Scott later wrote that, in early December 1911, Lloyd George had talked of a plan in which Henderson and sixty other M.P.s were '. . . all prepared to take part in a Suffrage campaign in the country, and that after the outrages began the whole thing came to a dead stop'. Lloyd George, in a speech to the Liberal Federation at Bath a few days after the Asquith declaration, noted that the fury of the militants—'those anti-Liberal women' arose because the wives of working men were to be enfranchised and this did not please 'the Tory can-

[7] Papers of Lord Haldane of Cloan, Scottish Nat. Library Mss. 6011, F. 170–1 Haldane to Elizabeth Haldane, 22 November 1911.

[8] Quoted in Pankhurst, Christabel, *Unshackled. The Story of How We Won The Vote* (Hutchinson, London, 1959), p. 191.

vasser'. Lloyd George was clearly preparing the ground both for an attack on militants and a campaign for Suffrage. On the other hand both Lloyd George and Grey had told Suffragists that their loyalty to Asquith prevented them forcing the inclusion of Suffrage, while Asquith gave his opinions frankly to the deputation from the Antis led by Lord Curzon. The split in the cabinet was public property.

There is evidence that opposition from Suffragists was, in fact, based on judicious estimates of the results of Asquith's declaration. By making franchise reform a party issue, and by stating his readiness to accept Suffrage, Asquith had split the Commons coalition majority over it. It was not unreasonable for Suffragists to have believed that Unionists anxious for Suffrage would now vote against it, since it was to be part of a government-sponsored virtual Adult Suffrage measure. Bonar Law, in a letter to Betty Balfour shortly after the delegation saw Asquith, showed signs of just this position. Noting that 'I have felt and feel strongly that women should not be deprived of votes on account of their sex' he went on to lament the demise of the Conciliation Bill 'for it might have settled the question for a long time . . .'. He was quite clear, however, that he was against any large extension of the franchise 'while there is in the country a distinct danger of a revolutionary movement'.[9] In this situation it was little wonder that militants assumed that this splitting was the government's intention—that in fact manhood suffrage was a classic, and very necessary, red herring if the government was not to be embarrassed by the Conciliation Bill.

What if, on the other hand, Lloyd George *had* been able to force the cabinet to face up to the problem of electoral reform, and if the non-inclusion of Suffrage in the bill was merely a mechanism to allow Asquith and his friends to save face? What if the cabinet was now set on pushing through Reform and Redistribution—Ireland being protected by the parallel passage of Home Rule? If this were possible, there should be evidence of very

[9] Papers of Andrew Bonar Law 26/1/72, Bonar Law to Lady Betty Balfour, 11 November 1911.

real strain in the cabinet, and evidence of resentment against militants for endangering Liberal plans.

Churchill, at least, was highly alarmed by the developing situation. In mid-December he had, in a letter to Lloyd George, deplored the 'mawkish frenzy' that he and Grey were in and added that if they pressed the enfranchising of '8,000,000 Women *without a fresh appeal to country* . . . I could not find any good foothold for common action . . . I could not go with you in a campaign . . . which would not be for the good of the country.'[10]

On 18 December he was even more eloquent to the Master of Elibank.

we are getting into vy gt peril over Female Suffrage. Be quite sure of this—the Franchise Bill will not get through without a dissolution if it contains a clause adding 8,000,000 women to the electorate. Nor ought it to get through.

How can the P.M. honourably use the Parliament Act to force it upon the King, when he has himself declared it to be a 'disastrous mistake'? In the record year of passage of this and the Home Rule Bill, the Tories will demand a dissolution. Votes for women is so unpopular that by-elections will be unfavourable. The King will be entitled . . . to dismiss the Ministry and Parliament will be dissolved on the old Plural Voting Register. We shall be in confusion ourselves. With us will go down the Irish cause.

The situation which is developing is vy like the Trade split in the Tory Party in 1903. I do not understand L.G. at all. Their one hope was the referendum wh alone gave a reasonable and honourable outlet. He knew my view. And yet he has gone out of the way to rule it out at the vy beginning . . .

What a ridiculous tragedy it would be if this strong Government and Party . . . was to go down on Petticoat politics. And the last chance of Ireland—our loyal friends squandered too! It is damnable.

No doubt you have made some deep calculations as to voting in the H of C . . . But I do not think there is any safety there. If L.G.

[10] Papers of Earl Lloyd George of Dwyfor c/3/15/12, Churchill to Lloyd George, 16 December 1911.

87

and Grey go on working themselves up, they have to go if Female Suffrage is knocked out. And the PM's position will become impossible if it is put in.

The only safe and honest course is to have a referendum—first to the women to know if they want it, and then to the men to know if they will give it . . .'[11]

Two days later he penned the substance of this letter in a note to Grey, adding that if he and Lloyd George came to see Suffrage as '. . . the only question in politics . . . you will find it very difficult to regard me as anything but an opponent'.[12]

That night he, Grey, and Lloyd George dined together to discuss the matter. The following day he reported to Asquith that they had come to an understanding that, if the 'democratic' (Grey) amendment was carried then, after the new register had been created, women should be asked '. . . by referendum or initiative . . . whether . . . they wd take up their responsibilities or not.' He went on

In order to get them (Grey & LG) to adopt this position, I shd have to go with them on the democratic amendment, so that we cd all work together; & I am bound to say that any objections to the change wd be greatly diminished if 3 or 4,000,000 women, representing as they wd every household in the country, had specifically asked for it. Also, it wd probably get smashed wh again wd be a solution.[13]

The following day Asquith replied. He noted that he might '. . . feel it my duty . . .' to go to the large Anti-Suffrage demonstration being planned for the Albert Hall on 28 February. He went on 'I am clear that the Govt as a Govt, could not take any other course than we have taken. The only alternative was for the minority among us to resign . . . I reserve my judgement as to the

[11] Elibank Papers Folder 2B, Churchill to Elibank, 18 December 1911.

[12] Churchill, Randolph S., *Winston S. Churchill* (Heinemann, London, 1969), Vol. II, Companion, Part III, 1911–14. Churchill to Grey, 20 December 1911, p. 1474.

[13] *Ibid.*, Churchill to Asquith, 21 December 1911, pp. 1475–6.

practicability of your referendum until I have further considered it. As I understand, you propose that only the women should be referees? Why?"[14]

As the new year began the tension continued to rise. On 3 January the Master of Elibank replied to Churchill's letter of 18 December

It is certainly a most delicate situation, and the most difficult problem I have come up against since I have been Chief Whip . . . I am only concerned as to whether our party will gain by the inclusion or exclusion of women . . . I feel pretty certain that the suffrage will come; we can of course delay it.[15]

Compromise was not going to be easy. In mid-January a letter from Margot Asquith identified both the cabinet antagonists and the danger of disruption. Mrs. Asquith was hardly the most objective observer and caution is necessary in reading her opinions. Nevertheless, since other sources do not contradict her, her testimony gains in credence: '. . . you must never think I think L.G. disloyal to Henry. I think the reverse, but I think he is at times a little too hasty in pushing things. I agree that suffrage is the awkward thing, and will no doubt split us into smithereens unless you and H and L.G. and E. Grey get together and fix a referendum or something . . . I think it should be pointed out that the Unionist position on suffrage is exactly the same, but of course the answer to that is that they are not in office. H is logical but has been made ridiculous by all his colleagues . . . Once we admit the Referendum we really do start a Revolution. I should say Mrs. Fawcett's letter in Sat. *Times* was good. What we are being punished for is too many promises, and too much passion for popularity which means overloading the ship manned by men who are not fond of each other, all rather vain and very touchy— Loulou (counts for a little more not in weight but in rancour than you think, and should always be conciliated mildly) McK, J. Burns, Morley, Loreburn etc., the only thing they all agreed

---

[14] *Ibid.*, Asquith to Churchill, 23 December 1911, pp. 1476–7.
[15] *Ibid.*, Elibank to Churchill, 3 January 1912, pp. 1479–80.

on is Insurance, H Rule, Welsh Church?'[16] Two weeks later in two other letters, Mrs. Asquith spoke volumes for the mounting anxiety at No. 10 and the hope that the Master of Elibank, a friend of Lloyd George, could head him off. 'I'm against Winston's desire for Referendum over the d . . . . d women. We'd much better keep out of the Referendum, and think of some other way out—also use closure as little as possible in H Rule debates even if it means putting off one of our session's . . . measures . . . we must *all* stand and fall together, and as you say, if we can weather the W. Suffrage we shall be allright.' Again, the following day, 'Don't recommend the Referendum yourself, which is Winston's idea and the Westminster's. Every female would very properly say he had betrayed them. Let him stick to what he said and try to stop any more stumping. Don't let Loulou and McKenna speak in Albert Hall and add fuel to the flames. Henry's present position is hopeless and even ridiculous—he alone never saw the importance of enjoining silence on Grey and L George, and this fearful mistake will break us to a certainty. What a subject to smash over! Get L G and all of them to hold their tongues if possible. No P M would be placed in a worse position by colleagues and his own want of anxiety, than he is at the moment. Do all get together with sagacity and elasticity to get him out of it if you can—you are my one hope.'[17]

Mrs. Asquith's fears had probably been fed by the 'Strictly Confidential' letter which had arrived that morning from the Secretary of the Society of Certified and Associated Liberal Agents. This carried the view of the 350 English agents on the Franchise Bill. On the question of Woman Suffrage the District Meetings reported as shown on the opposite page.[18]

Both proponents and opponents of the issue could claim some support from this result. The survey did not give the voting fig-

[16] Elibank Papers, Folder 3, F. 4–7, Margot Asquith to Elibank, 14 January 1912.

[17] *Ibid.*, F. 8–9, 27 January 1912 and 28 January 1912.

[18] Society of Certified and Associated Liberal Agents, Minutes of Council, Vol. 4, 27 January 1912.

Area	Conciliation Bill	Married Women	All Women
Northern	Against	Against	In Favour
Midland	,,	,,	least detrimental
Yorkshire	,,	,,	In favour at 25 years old
Eastern	,,	,,	,, ,, ,,
Western	,,	,,	Against
S. Western	,,	,,	,,
Home Counties and London	,,	,,	,,
Lancs. and Cheshire	,,	,,	,,

ures for each area and thus it is impossible to obtain the overall majority view. Again, it is an open question whether the Agents may be taken as an accurate reflection of their respective areas and Liberal party members. Yorkshire, for example, is cited as being in favour of Woman Suffrage for all women over twenty-five years of age. Yet the Minutes of the Executive Committee of the Yorkshire Liberal Federation have nothing on the subject and conspicuously fail to mention it when later the Federation resolved to support the Franchise Bill. In the area of electoral reform the principal concern seemed to be with the plural voter—particularly after the two elections of 1910. The opinions of Liberal Agents on Woman Suffrage must, on this evidence alone, be viewed with caution. Lloyd George was *acting* on the assumption that a campaign within the party was a necessity.

For the moment, however, the potential disagreement in the party was much less significant than the tensions within the cabinet. Here, Woman Suffrage, for whatever reasons, was being championed by Lloyd George. In consequence, it had seemingly become capable of splitting the government when so much important legislation was pending. An issue which, in 1906, was peripheral to Liberal thinking looked, by early 1912, as if it might well divide the government when Liberal interests had become a legislative possibility. The Liberals had conquered the Lords only, it appeared, to fall before groups of window-breaking women. Mrs. Asquith was pardonably perturbed.

She was not alone. At the Labour Party Conference at

Birmingham a real struggle developed. Pressure on the executive had built up and had, perforce, to be dealt with. In 1907 Henderson had opposed risking Manhood Suffrage by entangling it with Woman Suffrage. Now he was in the position of having to move a resolution ' . . . that a bill which did not include women would be unacceptable to the great Labour and Socialist movement'. Snowden observed that there ' . . . were far more men who had votes, than there were men who could intelligently use those votes' while for the Miners, Robert Smillie declared that he was for Adult Suffrage, but opposed to refusing Manhood Suffrage if it was found impossible to include women. The Miners, however, were outvoted and the resolution was carried by 919,000 votes to 686,000.

It was this resolution that began the entente of the non-militant Suffragists and the Labour party. The militants noted, as Lady Constance Lytton wrote to Mrs. Fawcett, that the resolution was conditional on an end to militancy—and was therefore at most a gesture. Mrs. Fawcett, however, demurred and acted more positively. She was well aware of cabinet difficulties. Lady Frances Balfour wrote on 10 February that 'I have little doubt that among the many difficulties of the Government is the attitude of Loreburn. He has announced resignation if the Government, as such, take any steps. Both Asquith and Haldane would like his shoes. I saw Spender again . . . I saw there was much concern and anxiety at the back of his mind.' In her reply, Mrs. Fawcett did not conceal her pessimism on the chances of Asquith keeping his pledges—'I am full of fears about our prospects and believe we shall probably be tricked again . . . If he [Asquith] . . . breaks . . . [the pledges] he will disgrace himself and his Government. Pray rub this in to Mr. Spender.'[19] Just days later Mrs. Pankhurst, after her return from the United States, announced the new policy of organized use of the stone—'the time honoured official political argument'. The very same day in Bristol Charles Hobhouse was asserting that the militants must be seen in perspective,

[19] Papers of M. G. Fawcett, Vol. 3, Lady Frances Balfour to Mrs. Fawcett, 10 February 1912, Mrs. Fawcett to Lady Balfour, 11 February 1912.

that nothing they had done resembled the militancy prior to the 1832 and 1867 Reform Bills.

In Cabinet the debate continued. On 14 February Asquith reported to the King that 'Proposals will be brought forward for the amendment of the law with respect to the Franchise and the Registration of electors.' The Cabinet Committee considering the bill was hard at it. Herbert Samuel writing to John Burns a few days later plied him with a mass of queries on technicalities of registration which 'would not alter the proportion of one sex to another, which for our purpose is the most important thing'. By 24 February a draft existed of a Franchise and Registration Bill which granted the vote at twenty-three to male and female residents— including lodgers—in local government elections, but males only in parliamentary elections. It abolished the nine university seats, ended plural voting and established a process of continuous registration.

Among Conservatives the question, too, had acquired new life. If the government seriously intended Manhood—or even possibly Adult—Suffrage, then no politician could ignore the question. New voters and boundary changes concentrate the minds of politicians wonderfully. Austen Chamberlain in letters to his stepmother gives glimpses of the contenders of a bitter battle. 'F. E. Smith tells me that Willie Redmond's language about Lloyd George is unprintable. Redmond and his friends thought that, having helped the government to get the Veto out of the way, they would proceed on a straight course without any disturbing element to Home Rule. Now he says Lloyd George has queered the pitch, completely altered the situation, and jeopardized the success of Home Rule by the unpopularity of his Insurance Measure.

'It is reported that they have had some stormy meetings of the cabinet on the suffrage question. It appears that Asquith's statement about Adult Suffrage was made without any previous consultation with the cabinet—in this Government it appears that the Prime Minister at any rate is not allowed to declare a policy until it has received the assent of his colleagues. Meanwhile the

Suffragists in the cabinet are very angry with those of their colleagues who are to take part in the Albert Hall meeting, but I hear that Asquith turned fiercely on Lloyd George and told him that it was all his fault for trying to commit the Government and the Party at his Bath meeting. It seems quite likely that the Franchise Bill will never get presented, and that the Government will confine itself to producing a Plural Voting Bill, and giving time for the reconsideration of the Conciliation Bill. Robbins, however, suggested to me that the Government already begin to feel that they may get into such difficulties that they will be beaten on something, and if so, they may produce an Adult Suffrage Bill, and ride for a fall on the Women's Franchise in the belief that, as we are as much divided as themselves upon that subject, it would be the least favourable issue from which we could proceed to a dissolution.'[20] The same source confirms that Loreburn was in close support of Asquith in the contest with Lloyd George. 'F. E. Smith attended a meeting in the Lord Chancellor's room to discuss the speeches they would make at the Anti-Suffrage demonstration in the Albert Hall. He said he found the Lord Chancellor boiling with rage. "I shall say," said the Lord Chancellor, "that to pass such a measure without the clear sanction of the country, would be a great outrage on the Constitution." He added that he saw an attempt made in some quarters to twist the Prime Minister's words into meaning that if a Women's Suffrage amendment were inserted in the government Franchise Bill, it would thereafter have the whole force of the government behind it. "That", said the Lord Chancellor, "is not the case. I can name seven of my colleagues who will oppose it, and I myself will, in committee, in the House of Lords put down obstructive amendments." '[21] Chamberlain, as an active Anti-Suffragist, rejoiced in the spectacle of this cabinet disunity. The Antis, sensing that the conflict was coming to a head had, in early 1912, merged their

[20] Papers of Austen Chamberlain AC 4/1/741 Austen Chamberlain to Mrs. May Chamberlain, 14 February 1912.

[21] Chamberlain, Austen, *Politics From the Inside* (Cassell and Co. London, 1936), p. 423.

organizations for men and women under Curzon and were extremely active. After the huge meeting at the Albert Hall on 29 February, Chamberlain wrote to his stepmother that, 'Loulou on his colleagues was also very interesting, (as was) . . . Loreburn on a "constitutional outrage". I had a few words with Mr. Harcourt afterwards. It is evident they are furious with Lloyd George.'

For the moment anyway, Lloyd George was with the Anti-Suffragists in opposing the coming Conciliation Bill. Speaking at the Albert Hall on 23 February, he had reaffirmed his opposition. '. . . if I were convinced that, owing to Parliamentary difficulties, no other measure was possible, I should certainly support, much as I dislike it, even the Conciliation Bill. But I am not convinced. In our colonies, in the United States of America, in Norway, the franchise has been conceded upon broad democratic principles, and I am firmly convinced that . . . we shall be able to carry it this year.'

The Conciliation Bill had been reintroduced just over a week before. Mrs. Pankhurst had announced that the Women's Social and Political Union were no longer interested in a bill which had already been killed in advance. She further announced a campaign of window smashing set to begin on 1 March. A week after Lloyd George had spoken at the Albert Hall the West End resounded with the smashing and splintering of hundreds of shop windows. Relays of women descended on Piccadilly, the Haymarket, Oxford Street and Bond Street making the situation quite beyond police capacity to contain, far less prevent. To make the point—if this were needed—Mrs. Pankhurst drove to Downing Street and, before being arrested, she managed to put four stones through the windows of No. 10. With the Miners beginning their long-threatened strike the same day the government nerved itself for strong measures. By 4 March, Harcourt could write to Herbert Gladstone 'I am quite hopeful of defeating their Conciliation Bill . . . largely owing to the folly of their proceedings.' That same day, as hundreds of policemen were waiting in Parliament Square for a demonstration which never came, dozens of women descended on Knightsbridge and in minutes, amidst the sounds of shattering windows, made their protest and then escaped. The government now had its chance and took it. On 5 March the Pankhurst offices were raided and Mr. and Mrs. Pethick-Lawrence were arrested on conspiracy charges. Christabel escaped and from this point onward ran the WSPU from Paris, where she lived under the alias of Miss Amy Johnson. In the light of these events Hobhouse's speech a fortnight earlier, in which he had compared the intensity of the agitation unfavourably with that of 1832 and 1867, looks something like ministerial provocation.

If Antis in the cabinet had wanted cause to descend on the Pankhursts and destroy the Conciliation Bill, they had all they needed. So far as the chief protagonists were concerned, there appears to have been a crucial decision reached on 7 March. Lady Frances Balfour reported to Mrs. Fawcett, 'Betty reports that at Grillions on Monday, Cantuar, Haldane, Grey and Asquith all agreed nothing more could be done this session for suffrage. Asquith told them the police believed that there was a plot to assassinate Lloyd George. Betty says she knows Lloyd George threatened resignation if a clause enabling women was not permitted in the Manhood Suffrage Bill. Asquith was so angry he would not speak to him for some days.'[22] That clash, however, could be postponed while both sides co-operated in fulfilling the government's pledge of time for the Conciliation Bill. On 14 March there had been a meeting of Anti-Suffrage M.P.s. Austen Chamberlain, who was clearly co-operating closely with Harcourt, noted to his stepmother 'It is estimated that in our Party there are 110 absolutely trustworthy Anti-Suffragists and 70 convinced Suffragists. This leaves 95 doubtfuls, of whom I dare say as many as 30 will vote for us and a good many more will not vote at all. The return of the Liberal Party is far less satisfactory. They have a great majority of supporters of the cause, but Harcourt is very busy lobbying among them with good results. He is made for that kind of work which I cannot endure. He is pretty

[22] Fawcett Papers, Vol. 3, Lady F. Balfour to Mrs. Fawcett, 7 March 1912.

confident that he can get a large number of the Irish to vote against the Bill and he is hard at work intriguing with them. No doubt what he says to them is that if the Bill gets past a Second Reading, and the Government in accordance with their pledge have to find time for it, it will seriously jeopardise the prospects of Home Rule.'[23]

While Mr. and Mrs. Pethick-Lawrence and Mrs. Pankhurst, released on bail, prepared their defence for the coming trial, the doomed Conciliation Bill was brought to its Second Reading on 28 March. The Pankhurst organization in open hostility prepared itself for the bill's defeat, while the non-militants, aware of parliamentary manoeuvring, sought a last-minute postponement. At this stage, there was no cabinet disunity. Suffragists there could join Anti-Suffragists in opposition to the bill. Besides, as a very sceptical Henry Norman wrote to the Master of Elibank on the subject of ministerial threats of resignation, 'My own view, rather, is that among men in good health drawing £5,000 a year, some die (and *that* rarely), but none resign.'

The *Manchester Guardian*, of 27 March, carried appeals for support from non-militant Suffrage organizations and from the Women's Liberal Federation. The Fabian Women's Group Executive tried to pacify the Labour party and suffragist Liberals by noting that 'a large majority for this small instalment of the Franchise, will urge on the Liberal Party to make sure of a bigger measure which would be more useful to them electorally'. On the morning of the debate, *The Times* had an editorial noting that the bill affronted Conservative assertions that the Constitution was in abeyance, and went on, 'With what consistency can they support a Constitutional revolution which goes deeper than Welsh Disestablishment, or even Home Rule?' The same issue carried a violent letter from the bacteriologist Sir Almroth Wright. In three columns he attacked the participation of women in politics from the physiological viewpoint, and castigated militants as essentially immoral and sexually embittered women. The

[23] Chamberlain Papers. AC 4/1/786 Austen Chamberlain to Mrs. May Chamberlain, 14 March 1912.

Manchester Guardian, the same day, reported that the National-ists had been notified by the Irishwomen's Suffrage Federation to the effect that, since the coming Home Rule Bill contained no security for the inclusion of Suffrage, Nationalist opposition to the establishment of the principle via the Conciliation Bill would be 'an act of hostility to Irish women', who would naturally thereafter put Suffrage before Home Rule.

The debate itself lasted six and a half hours. Proponents tried to minimize the significance of militancy by citing the opposition of the Pankhursts to the bill. Opponents took the other side, stress-ing that militancy was the very proof of unfitness for the parlia-mentary vote, and certainly for parliamentary membership which they saw as an immediate consequence of enfranchisement. On dividing the Commons rejected the bill by 257 to 243 with pairs. By a majority of 14 the government was free of the albatross which had hung around its neck for two years. Prior to the vote it is clear that some of the Conservative Antis wished the bill to pass so as, subsequently, to take more government time in the Commons. Austen Chamberlain refused to acquiesce in this gam-bit 'whilst recognising the party advantage'. He felt it would 'not be loyal to Harcourt and other Liberals who have fought the battle strenuously . . .' His scruples did him credit, though on his own evidence many of his friends had few scruples as they voted. 'There was much excitement during the division. Both sides thought the Pros had won, and it was said towards the end of the debate that their majority would be as much as 50. We were just out of our lobby, and when we saw our members were 222 we knew it would be a close division . . . Several men were in a des-perate hurry to catch the night mails to the country—indeed the Closure division was deliberately engineered by some of the Antis in the belief that 8 or 9 Pros would be obliged to go before the second division was called. But the figures in the second division don't show any falling off. On the contrary they are higher than in the first, but it is just possible that some men voted but did not get marked.'[24]

[24] Chamberlain, Austen, *op. cit.*, pp. 466–7.

This explanation of the failure of the proponents was discounted in the press the following day. *The Times*' parliamentary correspondent wrote of the 'prearranged vote of the Nationalists and bitter resentment . . . expressed by Liberal supporters of the Bill . . . Mr. John Redmond at the last Party meeting let it be known that he was going to vote against the bill. The Nationalists voted accordingly.' The *Manchester Guardian*'s correspondent was less inclined to lay the blame solely at Redmond's door. He did note that the Irish 'did not want anything to stand in the way of the Home Rule Bill, and they are determined to say so quite clearly in the division lobby'. He went on, however, to note that eighteen miners' M.P.s were absent, and that Asquith's known hostility was important. The parlousness of Liberal fortunes, he claimed, meant that, 'Only those Liberals most strongly convinced . . . now feel justified in going into the lobby against him' *The Times* the following day carried the statement of Mrs. Fawcett's National Union which analysed the failure. This sought to show that the fourteen votes need not only have been Irish. Thirteen miners' M.P.s, it claimed, were absent because of the coal strike, while Anti efforts had succeeded in leading fifteen Liberals and ten Unionists to break their pledges as a gesture against militancy.

The National Union with its eyes on the coming Manhood Suffrage Bill was here trying to offend the Irish as little as possible —not all its membership strove to be as equable. The relief at No. 10 was apparent in the letter of Asquith to the Master of Elibank of 30 March: 'I think we are now nearly out of the wood.' Churchill, too, wrote to the Master in a mood of relief tempered, however, by the prospect of the difficulties implicit in legislation the government was embarked upon. 'A most difficult task lies before you between now and Christmas. I do not believe any Parliamentary difficulties of a serious character will arise, but by-elections will continue for the next eighteen months to be a source of great peril and vexation.' Woman Suffrage had been disposed of for the moment. The window-smashing campaign had opened the Pankhursts to the charge of conspiracy and Mrs.

Pankhurst and the Pethick-Lawrences had been given nine month sentences, and costs against them.

While Suffragists looked to the proposed Manhood Suffrage Bill, the government turned elsewhere. On 11 April it introduced its Home Rule Bill and, the followng day, its Bill for Welsh Disestablishment. Haldane's comment was to prove apt. 'The Home Rule business is now on us with full fury, and it will want much resolution.' The cabinet, however, could not escape concerning itself with the proposed Manhood Bill. On 25 April Asquith, in his report to the King noted, 'Mr. Pease reported the results of the deliberations of the Cabinet Committee which has been in charge of the question for some months.' The substance of its recommendations was concerned chiefly with registration though, to secure the new 'lodger' vote, a residential qualification was to be added to the household qualification. Asquith went on, 'These changes were approved by the Cabinet. It is estimated that their effect may be to increase the number of adult votes from 8,000,000—the present figure—to about 9,500,000. It was agreed that such an extension of the electorate must be followed by a redistribution of electoral areas. Several points of detail were referred back to the committee for further consideration.' On 17 May the cabinet 'discussed . . . some details arising out of the proposed franchise legislation'. Three days earlier a new draft Franchise and Registration Bill had been circulated. The Committee had run into great difficulty in trying to include changes in the local government franchise, and had decided to leave it 'exactly as it is' and concentrate on the parliamentary franchise and the abolition of the university seats. In the process, therefore, of refining the bill a proposal which would have given a number of married women the local government franchise had been dropped.

On 4 June Loreburn resigned the Lord Chancellorship on grounds of ill-health and was replaced by Haldane. One of the strongest opponents of Suffrage had left the Cabinet on the eve of the commencement of what promised to be a momentous few months. Suffrage—even the current unlikely compromise—had been yet another source of great disagreement between Loreburn and a Cabinet 'increasingly dominated by Liberal Imperialists'.[25] Haldane was now even better placed to help Suffrage, if he wished.

By June 1912, Woman Suffrage was beginning to assume its pre-1914 importance as a political question. Back in 1906, it had been a peripheral issue; by 1912 it had become if not a front rank then certainly a second rank topic for consideration. It had hastened and broadened the Liberal cabinet consideration of unfinished franchise business. But that same cabinet was fearfully split, if only because the Prime Minister himself seemed adamantly opposed to any measure at all, and certainly to all those proposed. Now, in June, there had begun what he himself had said was Suffrage's best opportunity to succeed. But was this his real opinion when he continued to declare his hostility? Could a Prime Minister allow a course such as was proposed to succeed and, after the Conciliation Bill vote in March, would it succeed anyway? The first reading of the government bill was due to take place on 17 June. Amid a divided party and cabinet and a tense political situation, few could not believe that a political Pandora's Box would be opened.

[25] Koss, S. E., Lord Haldane, *Scapegoat for Liberalism* (Columbia U.P., 1969), p. 95.

VIII.   Many a Slip Twixt...

*I put it to him that it would be a horrible
position for Home Rulers like myself to be
torn between our allegiance to Home Rule,
and our determination to resist the ruin of
the Suffrage cause . . .*
C. P. Scott to John Redmond, 20 January 1913.

*In Mr. Asquith's opinion . . . the Speaker's
judgement is entirely wrong.*
Mr. Asquith to H.M. the King,
24 January 1913.

1912 promised to be as hectic as 1911. The government had on
its hands two major pieces of legislation—the Home Rule and
Welsh Disestablishment Bills—and was soon to introduce its
Franchise and Registration Bill. Given the logic of the Parliament
Act and the necessity to keep all three bills to their timetables—
the Liberals could expect hard work and tight whipping. All three
bills had created dissension in the party and serious contention
with the Opposition. Meanwhile, restiveness in the Labour movement had not subsided and, on the Suffrage front, an escalation
of militancy was clearly expected if the Franchise Bill offered
nothing on Suffrage. As it was, ministers could make only heavily
guarded public appearances and there were rumours of possible assaults on their families. In late May there began a long
and very bitter dock strike in London, which was deeply pre-
occupying ministers as the Franchise Bill was read for the first
time on 18 June.

   The Times did not approve of the Franchise and Registration

Bill, declaring editorially that 'Redistribution is far more urgently wanted even than a simplification of franchise law if the object is to obtain a more complete and true expression of the national will.' It concluded that the bill was 'an attempt to gerrymander the existing constituencies in the interests, or supposed interests, of the party in power'. Its Lobby Correspondent, citing a government source, claimed that the bill was merely a fulfilment of Asquith's pledge, was meant to be defeated on the Suffrage issue and so would allow the government to adopt a simple plural voting bill. In view of the sequel to the bill, this was somewhat prescient reporting, though it probably represented no more than Unionist opinion in the Commons. It represented, too, the hope and intention of some of the Liberals who took Asquith's position. It did not, however, satisfy Lloyd George and he, as Samuel wrote to Herbert Gladstone on 23 June, was 'tired but still has the party in his grip ... [and was getting Welsh Disestablishment though it was] ... thoroughly disliked by our own party, and English Nonconformity shows no enthusiasm for it.'[1] A man that well positioned would have to be conciliated somehow.

The bill was down for Second Reading on 12 July. Pease had been in charge of it in June; Harcourt was to be now—both were hostile to Suffrage. On 2 July the Labour party executive had accepted a resolution by Ramsay MacDonald urging acceptance from Mrs. Fawcett's National Union of a 'sum of money for the specific object of supporting individual candidates in any constituency where Liberal Anti-Suffragists may be successfully opposed, and that the Union also support such candidates by the organization of a vigorous campaign on their behalf'.[2] This open alliance of a basically Liberal organization with the Labour party only strengthened the impression of discord between the government and its women supporters. The Women's Liberal Federation, on 4 June, had resolved that, unless the bill did enfranchise

---

[1] Papers of Herbert, Viscount Gladstone, B.M. Add. Mss. 45992, F. 269. H. Samuel to Gladstone, 23 June 1912.

[2] Papers of the Labour Representation Committee, *Infancy of Labour*, Vol. 2, Folios 307–8.

women, amicable relations with the party would become 'perhaps impossible'.

A week before the Second Reading, on 5 July, the cabinet considered its legislative timetable for the next session and Pease was asked to prepare detailed schedules for each of the three major bills. He was also asked by Asquith, for reasons of parliamentary time, to think of moving the Franchise Bill to 1913 'in the hope that we could secure its passage by means of the Parliamentary Bill in 1915 in our last possible session'. Pease replied that, after Asquith and Elibank's pledges, to do so would increase the possibility 'of the return of another government pledged to protective tariffs . . .'[3] One man, at least, came away from the cabinet meeting with a clear picture of the primary intention of the Franchise Bill. John Burns recorded in his Diary 'Cabinet. Disenfranchisement'.[4] If Asquith could fulfil the November 1911 pledge to both Adult and Woman Suffragists, and then defeat the women, all well and good. If the bill ended plural voting and created a lodger vote amenable to the Liberals, then better still. But, at the very least, the government would end plural voting either in this, or another bill. In one word, Burns had summed up the probable expectation of the bulk of the cabinet.

Asquith's speech in the Second Reading debate must be seen in this light. The defeat of the Conciliation Bill, he claimed, had been of 'sufficient decisiveness' as to be final on the question of Suffrage for the moment. He went on '. . . I dismiss at this moment as altogether improbable the hypothesis that the House of Commons is likely to stultify itself by reversing . . . the considered judgement at which it has already arrived.'

The response of the militants to Asquith's confident rejection went beyond brawling in Parliament Square and smashing windows in Piccadilly and Regent Street. In June, after the First Reading, the Prime Minister was forcibly accosted by Suffragettes at an India Office Reception; in July he was assaulted at a

[3] Papers of Walter Runciman, WR 68, J.A. Pease to Runciman, 6 July 1912.
[4] The Papers of John Burns, B.M. Add. Mss. 46334, *Diary 1912*, 5 July.

private reception given by his brother-in-law. His speech on the Second Reading snapped such constraints as had existed in militant minds. A policeman foiled an attempt to burn down Harcourt's home. Asquith, in Dublin, was narrowly missed and Redmond hit by a hatchet tossed by Mrs. Mary Leigh into their open carriage. Not satisfied with this gesture, Mrs. Leigh that evening tried to burn down the empty Theatre Royal and, in due course, was sentenced to five years' penal servitude. In September Lloyd George narrowly escaped a whipping at the hands of Suffragettes who found him playing golf at Llanystumdwy. Cabinet ministers, long used to witnessing the painful, noisy ejections of Suffragist hecklers, now had to consider their public appearances as distinctly hazardous. The Royal Family itself was not immune—Suffragettes hoisted Women's Social and Political Union flags on the golf course at Balmoral and painted slogans on a nearby fountain!

Months earlier, H. N. Brailsford had laid out the parliamentary position as seen by the Suffragist Liberals and non-militant Suffragists. In a National Union pamphlet he noted that the bill re-enacted the local government franchise qualifications as they stood: thus, in effect solidifying the disenfranchisement of married women in the English boroughs and counties, and preventing Suffragists from uniting behind a simple amendment enfranchising women on the local government register. The debate then, he concluded, would have to centre on an amendment enfranchising both householders and wives of householders—a ridiculous situation if wives were disfranchised on the local government register. The plan of the anti-suffrage wing of the cabinet was only too obvious—the amendment would have to be carried by Irish votes. Redmond, '. . . holds the balance, at any event, for any democratic solution. There is every reason to fear that it is his intention, from some sense of obligation to the anti-suffrage wing of the cabinet, to repeat the manoeuvre by which the Conciliation Bill was defeated. He will fling forty, or even sixty votes against every suffragist amendment, and order his more decidedly suffragist followers once more to abstain. Liberals cannot disavow all responsibility for the acts of their ally while the coalition subsists. If the Liberal party allows Mr. Redmond to put an Irish veto on the enfranchisement of English women, it must be prepared to share the odium of his intervention.'[5]

The Irish, then, held the key so far as many Suffragists were concerned—and by 1912 they were unlikely to help. Bonar Law at Blenheim in late July, and developments in Ulster, which were to lead to the Ulster Covenant of September, promised bitter party conflict, if not worse. Redmond would do nothing to weaken the Liberals at this point. A letter of John Galsworthy to Mrs. Fawcett seems to indicate that, privately, the National Union had given up the Reform Bill, and that their policy of alliance with Labour was intended not to coerce the Liberals immediately by a future threat, but rather to give Labour the balance of power at the next election. Further evidence of despair is found in the behaviour of George Lansbury and, to a lesser extent, in that of Snowden. Lansbury, ever volatile, had caused uproar in the Commons in June when he had raged at the complacency of Asquith while Suffragettes languished in prison. By October, 1912, he was circularizing the Independent Labour Party, attacking its leadership, and demanding that it resolve to press for action on Suffrage and resist the Reform Bill. The Labour Party Executive, in committee with the parliamentary Labour party, resolved that '. . . the policy urged in the resolution is not in harmony with the decision of the Annual Conference of the party and, while recognizing that the procedure rules of the House often prevent votes being given solely on the merits of the issue to be decided, [the Executive] . . . is determined to press for the inclusion of women in the Franchise and Registration Bill.'[6]

On 5 November, with the Home Rule Bill in the Committee Stage, Philip Snowden tried to coerce the Nationalists by seeking to allow women to vote for the proposed Irish Parliament. Red-

[5] Brailsford, H. N., *Women and the Reform Bill* (NUWSS Pamphlet, London, December 1911).

[6] *Infancy of Labour, op. cit.*, Divisional Council No. 6, Minute Books 1909–16, 10 October 1912.

mond, understandably alarmed, asked that the question be left to the Irish people, and met the rejoinder that if the Franchise Bill did include women then Irish women would already be enfranchised. The government had to put on Whips to ensure that this move would be defeated—even so, thirty Liberals voted for the motion. Woman Suffrage was, once again, thoroughly entangled with the Irish Question.

The crescendo of militancy and the seemingly inevitable extension to arson had the effect of forcing the Pethick-Lawrences to consider their position inside the WSPU. Between August and October 1912 they tried to urge a pause, were overridden and then were actually expelled from the WSPU by the imperious Christabel Pankhurst. Though they continued to produce *Votes for Women* their caution was missed, and the WSPU was delivered into the hands of a leader who ran it from Paris and an increasingly disparate following unready to accept most forms of control.

The behaviour of Lansbury must be seen against this background of the fear of Suffragists over the plight of their movement in such hands. On 11 November, he announced his resignation from the Commons and, two days later, his resignation from the Labour party. He offered himself for re-election at Bow and Bromley on a Suffrage platform. His election address noted that in March, in the Conciliation Bill division, Liberals and Irish had swung over because '. . . if this bill had been carried certain ministers would resign, and Home Rule would be endangered. We have no guarantee that such Members will not act in the same way on the Government's Franchise Bill.' The electors of Bow listened but were not persuaded, and Lansbury's gesture ended in his decisive defeat. The WSPU had, with the other Woman Suffrage organizations, campaigned for Lansbury. When, however, following his defeat, the various organizations were dismantled Sylvia Pankhurst remained behind and went on to form the London Suffrage Federation which was Socialist in complexion and democratic enough in organization to merit expulsion from the WSPU by Christabel Pankhurst within a little over a year.

Haldane was not alone in seeing the affair as indicating public displeasure with militancy. Neither he nor Lloyd George, however, were prepared to see the defeat as endorsing governmental inaction. Both would have argued that if the Liberal leadership threw its weight behind a campaign for suffrage such displeasure could be converted into public support for a solution to the problem which created militants. The mass of voters needed the guidance of the two major parties and this could not be given. When guidance was given during 1917 there was little public opposition.

The volatile Mr. Lansbury had, a month prior to his resignation, aired his convictions in another direction. On 11 October, in the debate on the Marconi contract, he had become the first M.P. to give public vent in the Commons to the suspicions that the contract involved scandal and corruption, and that ministers were implicated. The debate had led to a Select Committee being established to consider the contract and the circumstances of its granting. This sat through the latter weeks of 1912 providing the electors, via the press, with a seemingly endless stream of speculation and innuendo. This would have been weakening to any party in office. But to a Liberal government pressing Home Rule and Welsh Disestablishment in the face of very determined Unionist resistance, it was doubly so.

For Suffrage it was a disaster, since Lloyd George was directly involved. At a time when the government was pressing a Franchise Bill and was split on Suffrage, the only man with political force enough to secure the inclusion of Suffrage, and prevent the breakup of the government, was being embarrassed by charges of corruption. No account of the Suffrage débâcle in 1913 can be complete without the realization that in that period the personal fortunes of Lloyd George were on the decline. At the very time when his political instincts told him that the Liberals must break out of the sterility of coercion on Suffrage, he was a captive of the chief architect of that policy—the Prime Minister. It is of no small significance that, over the next two months, when Suffrage was in the forefront of politics, very little was heard from Lloyd

George. He was in no position to fight. The Marconi affair is the crucial backcloth to the struggle that, at least in public, went on to amend the government's Franchise Bill due for further consideration in January.

On 21 November Asquith reported to the King that the Home Rule and Marconi affairs had disrupted the timetable of legislation. 'The best estimate that can now be formed . . . [allowing for the Christmas adjournment] . . . is that the Irish Bill may be sent to the House of Lords about January 9, the Welsh Bill about 29 January, and the Franchise Bill sometime about the 8th of February.'[7] Probably dating from this period is an undated 'Secret' memo sent to Harcourt by J. A. Pease, who had been in charge of the bill in June. This detailed the precautions necessary before using the guillotine on the bill to prevent Conservative obstruction and force the question of Suffrage to be decided. Pease then went on to press the notion that in Committee the bill could be stripped of all but its Plural Voter clauses, thus making it much more manageable[8]—and palatable to the Antis. The main reason he gave for this was truly ironic in view of subsequent events. He quoted Erskine May to support his belief in 'the practical certainty that the Speaker would rule, when the Bill came back from the Committee, that the Bill had been so altered as to compel the Government to introduce another Measure'.[9] The procedural problem for the government was clear. Now that they had published their bill, and had it read a second time, they had to try to carry it, increasingly hard though they found this. The bill might have a Suffrage amendment added; and it raised problems over the question of a simple residence qualification. Yet any attempt to cut the bill back to a simple Plural Voter Bill at the Committee Stage ran the risk of the Speaker forcing its withdrawal.

[7] Papers of the Earl of Oxford and Asquith, Vol. 6, F. 182–3. Asquith to H.M. the King, 21 November 1912.

[8] A suggestion made to Pease by the Executive Committee of the National Liberal Federation on 9 October. See the Papers of Lewis, Viscount Harcourt, LH 11/2.

[9] Harcourt Papers LH 11/2 Envelope, Franchise and Registration, Memo 'Franchise and Registration 1912'.

The impending embarrassment was clear to those on the periphery of the government circle. Writing to Grey, on 29 November, C. P. Scott asked for a denial of rumours that Asquith would resign rather than accept Woman Suffrage. Grey replied at once, denying the fears expressed and added 'It is only on the assumption that, if women's suffrage is put into the Bill the Government, which term of course includes the Prime Minister, will accept the decision, that I can promise in advance to accept the decision of the House, and to continue to support the Bill, if Women's Suffrage is not put into it.'[10] On 4 December, speaking to the National Conference of Mrs. Fawcett's National Union, Sir John Simon defended the coming bill and asserted that it was capable of having Suffrage inserted. 'Not only so ... but since I had something to do with the drafting of it, I may point out this further, that this Bill is so drafted that this very question . . . is bound to come up on the first page, on the first clause.'[11]

The day following this flat statement, as if to check on its validity, C. P. Scott wrote to Asquith. 'You undertook that the whole matter should be left to the unfettered judgement of the House, without respect to Party, and that the Government would accept and act upon its decision, whatever this might be. But, if there were reason to suppose that you would regard your personal position as being involved in the decision, then clearly the question would not be an open one. The whole weight both of party interests and of personal attachment to yourself, would be thrown into the scale and there can be no doubt which way it would tip . . .' The reply he received on 10 December was hardly reassuring. 'I do not feel called upon to take any notice of the rumours to which you refer, and which are circulated without my authority. My declarations, as head of the Government, as to what the attitude of the Government will be ... are ... perfectly

[10] Hammond, J. L., *C. P. Scott* (G. Bell and Sons, London, 1934), pp. 113–14.
[11] Simon, Sir John, *Speech at the National Delegates Meeting of the Women's Liberal Federation* (WLF Pamphlet, London, 1912).

plain and consistent. But I feel bound to add this. Some of my most valued colleagues and friends, such as the Lord Chancellor and Sir Edward Grey, are active promoters of Woman Suffrage . . . In these circumstances, holding the views I do hold, I cannot regard myself (as an individual) as being under any obligation to adopt a purely passive part, or to conceal in any way my opinion on the merits of the question from friends who are interested in knowing them.'[12]

It is as well to note, at this stage, the progress of the Home Rule Bill. In the Committee Stage the subject of redistribution in Ireland had been carefully skirted by the government. The government, assuming that the bill would need the Parliament Act, did not anticipate touching the problem of Irish redistribution. As Redmond pointed out to the Bishop of Raphoe, who had objected to Trinity College, Dublin being represented via the Home Rule Bill, 'The Government have avoided the creation of new constituencies in order to avoid the necessity of a redistribution Bill and a Boundary Commission, preferring, as I think wisely, to leave this matter in the hands of the Irish Parliament in the future.'[13] The Franchise Bill would give electoral advantage to the Liberals, and the Irish could settle their own redistribution —after Home Rule. The pressure on the government stemming from Home Rule was so great, however, that despite its carefully drawn timetables giving passage of Home Rule and Franchise Reform before an election, thoughts of earlier dissolution clearly had come to mind. On Christmas Day, Lloyd George was replying to Asquith on the subject of a spring election. The Chancellor was, it seems, a little concerned at the suggestion. He agreed that the election, if it must come early, must be held whilst trade boomed. He pointed out, however, that trade seemed set for at least another twelve months and, more importantly, urged that 'the three Bills' be sent to the Lords a second time before

[12] Hammond, *op. cit.*, p. 114.
[13] The papers of John Redmond, Envelope 16, Folder 3. Redmond to the Most Reverend Dr. O'Donnell, 17 December 1912. Irish. Nat. Lib. Mss. 15,217 (3).

dissolution. This would free the new Parliament from spending too much time on 'stale questions'.[14]

Timetables were becoming daily more important as utterances on Ireland grew in number and violence. The year opened with the Carson proposal to exclude Ulster from the Home Rule Bill. January 1913 was spanned by the Third Reading of the Home Rule Bill on the 16th, and its defeat in the Lords on the 30th. This progress was not unconnected with the Franchise Bill.

The diary of John Burns, and the Prime Minister's reports to the King, provide some glimpses of the scene as viewed from cabinet level. Burns noted for 2 January that, at the cabinet's Franchise Bill Committee, Asquith was '. . . in a very good humour about the week's work . . . We took a turn about Residence and Occupation and I think, as Pease did, that we converted him and others.' The following day the inevitable redistribution was discussed, and Burns noted 'Redistribution Bill, order to prepare Bill and memo for P.M.' Five days later, Asquith was reporting to the King that Pease had been instructed to amend the Occupation and Registration clauses which 'will simplify the measure and greatly reduce its bulk'. Other aspects, however, were not to be changed before introduction. Asquith reported further discussion of 'the voting of soldiers, the age of qualification, the position of the City of London, the machinery of continuous registration'. On 16 January after the passage of Home Rule, Burns noted 'P.M. really happy and settled in the saddle comfortably, at last is in possession of the reins . . .'[15]

At this time of great stress, Asquith's evident good humour must have stemmed in part from his view of the general success of his legislative programme. It was probably not entirely unconnected with the prospect of not having Suffrage forced on him. On 20 January Burns noted 'M.P.'s discussing all aspects of Votes for Women. Feeling hardening against all amendments. The belief is that they will all be beaten in interests of Home Rule and other

[14] Asquith Papers, Miscellaneous Corres., F. 110–11, Lloyd George to Asquith, 25 December 1912.

[15] Burns Papers, *Diary*, Add. Mss. 46335, 2, 3, 8, 16 January 1913.

matters that have preceded this question.' C. P. Scott shared this feeling, and that very day had gone to Redmond. The discussion was frank and was clearly not meant for publication.

I put it to him it would be a horrible position for Home Rulers like myself to be torn between our allegiance to Home Rule and our determination to resist the ruin of the Suffrage cause—to desire the success of the Government on the one ground and its defeat on the other; but that undoubtedly, that was what would happen if the Suffrage amendments were defeated and the Bill afterwards persisted in—that moreover if they were defeated by Irish votes, we should feel that there had been a betrayal by the Home Rule party of the very principle of Home Rule and that emancipation for Irishmen had been purchased at the cost of its refusal for English women. Our allegiance would be shaken—our ardour cooled.

He admitted that he was conscious of this and he earnestly hoped that such a situation would not arise. At the same time, he had to look at the alternative. For the Prime Minister, who had denounced women's suffrage as a 'national disaster', to be compelled, not only to accept it, but to press it through under the exceptional powers of the Parliament Act, would be an impossible position. There was no mandate for it from the country, which could justify the use of the Parliament Act. I replied that Mr. Asquith could not have thought so, or he would not have given his pledge. R. replied that he could not imagine why he had given it, but, evidently, felt that at all events, he must be relieved from the necessity of fulfilling it.[16]

As a contemporary Suffragist observer noted 'Mr. Harcourt and Mr. Churchill had gone among Irish and Welsh members and used the threat of Asquith's resignation effectively.'[17]

The situation was, from the Prime Minister's viewpoint, well in hand. The Irish would serve both their own and his interests. The report to the King of 22 January might be termed an insurance policy against any Commons accident. 'Some discussion took place on the Franchise Bill, and on the possible acceptance or rejection of the various woman suffrage amendments. It was

[16] Hammond, J. L., *op. cit.*, pp. 115–16.
[17] Blease, Lyon, *The Emancipation of English Women* (David Nutt and Co., London, 1913), p. 291.

agreed that, whatever might be the decision of the House of Commons, the members of the Government holding diverse views would not regard the result of such decision this year as calling for their resignation of office.'[18]

That same day, a Wednesday, Burns noted in his Diary 'House agitated as to Monday's Vote. M.P.'s hardening against Parliament Bill being used for such a great change;'—the Irish might not be needed after all. Before the words had been written in Burns' diary, Bonar Law had visited the Speaker in his office. He came to claim that an insertion of Suffrage into the proposed Bill would so alter it as to oblige the Speaker to insist on its withdrawal after the Committee Stage. The following day—Thursday the 23rd—the Speaker passed to the government his view that, should the Bill emerge from Committee containing a Suffrage clause, he would be bound to insist on it being withdrawn and redrafted. Here was farce indeed. Burns, clearly not aware of what had happened, noted 'Speech on Franchise (if necessary) prepared . . . Groups of women with placards parading around Parliament. Deputations on M.P.'s. J.R. really concerned, and greatly disturbed at situation. D L G [Lloyd George] J K H [Keir Hardie] . . . in Smoke Room. What does that fortuitous concert of atoms portend? J R [Redmond] looked as if he had "his doots".'[19]

Despite the uncertainty, the Commons went ahead and the debate did not finish until 6 a.m. on the 24th. At 3 p.m. the Cabinet met. Asquith, reporting to the King, wrote:

This is a totally new view of the matter, which appears to have ocurred for the first time to the Speaker himself only two or three days ago, and is in flat contradiction of the assumptions upon which all parties in the House, hitherto, treated the Bill.

In Mr. Asquith's opinion, which is shared by some of the best authorities on procedure, the Speaker's judgement is entirely wrong and impossible to reconcile with what took place in the case of

[18] Asquith Papers, Vol. 7, F. 5, Asquith to H.M. the King, 22 January 1913.

[19] Burns Papers, *Diary*, 23 January 1913.

previous Franchise Bills in 1867 and 1884. But there is, practically, no right of appeal against the dictum of a Speaker in such matters.

In these circumstances it is felt, not without reason, by the supporters of Woman's Suffrage that they cannot be afforded under the present Bill the opportunity for a 'free' discussion and division on their cause which was promised by the Government.

The Government, on the other hand, having done everything in their power to fulfill their promise are, for the moment, disabled by the Speaker's ruling which was wholly unexpected, and for which they are in no way responsible.

The general feeling of the Cabinet was that the Bill should be withdrawn, but so much depends upon the nature of the statement to be made that further consideration of the matter was adjourned until Monday morning.[20]

Well might the decision be postponed—Bonar Law and the Speaker had upset Asquith's almost certain destruction of Suffrage. That night Haldane wrote to his mother that the situation was 'serious. It will create a most difficult situation—wholly unforseen. I have much fear for the prospect of the whole Bill now and this will hurt the Government.'[21] John Burns—present at the overnight debate—was less temperate in his diary. 'Woman Suffragists have by undisciplined action outside Commons and in Cabinet put back for many years their own cause. Tearing defeat. Grey has become almost obsessed by his fanatical adhesion to his cause which has reason for complaint against its supposed best friends. . .'

There must clearly have been harsh words in the cabinet, and certainly in the Smoking Room of the Commons. The bill was certainly an embarrassment to the government and, in terms of self-justification for ministers, it was preferable to accept the killing of Suffrage by an unexpected ruling of the Speaker than to have to engineer the defeat of tabled Suffrage amendments. But it was hardly edifying, and more importantly, withdrawal

[20] Asquith Papers, Vol. 7, F. 5, Asquith to H.M. the King, 24 January 1913.
[21] Papers of Viscount Haldane of Cloan, Scottish National Library Mss. 5989, Haldane to Mary Haldane, 24 January 1913.

of the bill threw out the legislative timetable. Grey, sensitive to honour, had probably threatened resignation while even the more flexible Lloyd George had allowed his frustrations to boil over. Burns, the following day, noted, 'A crisis in Government has been arrested, but the Woman's Movement has sustained a serious blow for which its packrams are to blame.'[22] Haldane, a proponent of a limited female enfranchisement, was less inclined to blame suffragists in and out of the Cabinet. 'We are much worried by the action of the Speaker . . . The situation is entirely of his creation, and I think he is much to blame.'[23]

Speaker Lowther, had, meanwhile, left for the weekend at Tring, the home of Lord Rothschild. In his memoirs, he notes that it was there that he finally decided on his ruling. It was, in the light of subsequent history, a rather unfortunate choice for that particular weekend. Lord Rothschild was the leading financial supporter of the Antis and many of his friends were generous in that cause. As a subsequent pamphlet published by no less than the Conservative and Unionist Women's Suffrage Association showed, the principal contributors formed a roll-call of bankers, coal and steel magnates and one brewer, Lord Iveagh. The opposition, in fact, resembled nothing if not a goodish cross section of Edwardian plutocracy, a charge made good use of by most Suffragists thereafter.[24]

On 27 January, a Monday, there was a cabinet meeting after which Asquith reported to the King—'After a full discussion of the situation . . . the Cabinet . . . was unanimous in holding (1) that any legislation in regard to Plural Voting must be deferred to next Session, and (2) that facilities for the reasonable use

[22] Burns Papers, *Diary*, 25 January 1913.
[23] Haldane Papers, F. 28–9, Haldane to Mary Haldane, 25 January 1913.
[24] Chance, Lady, *The Predominance of Men in the Anti Suffrage Finance and Organisation* (Cons. and Unionist Women's Suffrage Association, 1913). Some examples were: a. of financiers—Viscount Rothschild, Lord Astor, Lord Joicey, Sir Ernest Cassell, b. of coal barons—Earl of Durham, Lord Joicey, Sir Andrew Noble, c. of steel magnates—Lord Ridley and David Davies.

of Government time should be offered to a Private Member's Woman Suffrage Bill next Session, the members of the Government being free to vote as they pleased, and the Government assuming no responsibility then or thereafter, for the Bill, beyond the giving of the necessary time.'[25] That afternoon the same report was made to the Commons when, in reply to a question, the Speaker affirmed his position. Greeting Asquith's announcement of the withdrawal of the bill came the inevitable opposition shouts of 'Resign, Resign'. The Prime Minister is reported to have asked in surprise—'On Woman's Suffrage?'

The amused reply was something of a pose, for behind the scenes there had been a cabinet crisis. Burns in his Diary noted that the '. . . Radicals not pleased with the dropping of the Franchise Bill' and that seems to have been an understatement. Haldane was soothing to his mother, but very explicit to his sister, 'Sunday night's' was an important meeting. Said I should have to resign if we went back on the Suffrage arrangements, and L G said he would also. So we deputed him and Grey to see the P.M. in the morning. The P.M. behaved like an angel and managed yesterday's Cabinet admirably. The new place is a good one and should afford the cause as good a chance as it had before.' Two days later he noted 'The air is cleared a good deal'.[26]

The suspicion that Asquith had known what was coming must have been abroad at cabinet level. Yet Asquith probably could and did argue that he had no need of collusion with the Speaker. Given the party context of the proposals there would be no majority forthcoming for Suffrage inclusion anyway. Certainly he insisted then, and later, in his memoirs, that Suffrage was expected to come up at the Committee Stage—both front benches assumed it would do so. Again, it was no secret that many Liberals had suspicions of the Speaker's impartiality. Lloyd George seems to have taken the view that, whether the ruling was impartially

[25] Asquith Papers, Vol. 7, F. 9, Asquith to H.M. the King, 27 January 1913.
[26] Haldane Papers, Mss. 6012, F. 2, 3, 4, Haldane to Elizabeth Haldane, 28 and 30 January 1912.

correct or no, Bonar Law and the Tories for 'the second time in two months ... have let us out by a tactical blunder'. In any event infuriated Suffragists believed that the Speaker had colluded either with a Tory leader wishing to preserve the plural voter, or with a Prime Minister who badly needed to save his face and his party's unity.

At Lambeth, the Labour party was in Conference. The Speaker's ruling caused predictable *furor*. Snowden spoke in support of an amended resolution instructing the parliamentary party to oppose 'any Franchise Bill in which women are not included'. He went on 'There was no one with five minutes experience of the House of Commons who believed, for a single moment, that there was a ghost of a chance of six or eight million women being enfranchised by a Private Member's bill ... Because Mr. Asquith and Mr. Harcourt were opposed to votes for women, were their opinions to carry more weight than that of 400 elected representatives in the House of Commons?' The answer in the British party context was clearly 'yes', at least in the short run.

Thus ended the ill-fated Franchise Bill and with it, as it proved, the last pre-war chance of securing Suffrage. Mrs. Pankhurst, and her daughter Sylvia, were now teetering into martyrdom as the cycle of hunger strike, release and protest followed each other. Arson had by now become almost routine—ministers, police, and militants alike had come to see themselves as engaged in a guerrilla war of sorts, in which the deaths of combatants and bystanders could not now be far away. There had been times before when the manner in which Suffrage had been defeated was as hard to bear for militants as the defeat itself—but at no time was this more true than in January 1913. No militant could be expected to believe that the Speaker's intervention had been unexpected or unplanned. The public braced itself as club windows were smashed in London, the orchid house at Kew was wrecked, golf courses in Birmingham were attacked with acid. Fears were raised of even more startling events to come and with fear went frustration at police impotence. The government must *do* something and quickly.

For Suffragists who did not believe in collusion there was the alternative belief that, even if Suffrage had come to the vote, Asquith and Redmond together could have defeated it. The Speaker by his action acted as the lightning rod for Suffragist fury and Liberal frustration. With an election clearly not too distant, the Liberals had to rescue the Plural Voting clauses from the bill and, meanwhile, proceed with Home Rule and Welsh Disestablishment. There was much to do and, in Asquith's eyes, much that was more important than Suffrage. It had been a peripheral issue in 1906 and militancy and cabinet intrigue gave it, in his eyes, no increased standing. Indeed, quite the reverse was true and it was this feeling coming on top of political difficulty which prevented an honourable truce between Suffragists and the British Liberal party.

IX. Stalemate

*I can tell you quite honestly that no one was
more disappointed than I was, and no one
regretted it more than I did.*
Mr. Asquith to Suffragists, 8 August 1913.

*If the change has to come, we must face it
boldly and make it thoroughgoing and
democratic in its basis.*
*Mr. Asquith to East End Suffragists,
20 June 1914.*

The country buzzed over the embarrassment of the government,
the dubious nature of the Speaker's ruling, and the apparent inability of the government to draft its bills carefully enough. Yet
Asquith, of course, had cause to be cheerful. The Speaker, by
dispatching a complex and cumbersome bill, had saved parliamentary time, and more, had prevented what might have been a
dangerous situation had Suffrage been made a real issue during
the debate. Grey with his honour outraged, Lloyd George resent-
ful and fearful over Marconi, Harcourt with his vindictive anti-
suffrage attitudes—the three made a trio capable of shattering
delicate cabinet compromises and landing Asquith, the government, and the Liberal programme in unsought disaster. True,
the Liberals needed to disfranchise the Plural Voter—but that
could be achieved in a simpler bill. Equally true, the Suffragette
reaction was a nuisance and embarrassment—but did this not
damn Suffrage and might there not be some legislative method of
isolating and ruining the militants? The Home Rule and Welsh
Church Bills must now jointly be pressed by a united government,
and the timing of the next election considered.

The débâcle was, however, not seen in all Liberal quarters as an unmixed blessing. J. A. Spender, writing to Gladstone early in February noted 'The Government here has had a decided recovery and, except for the woman suffrage fiasco, the session has been smooth. That question is going to be very troublesome, and may have a real (and incalculable) effect on the next election. If the Bill promised for the next session passes the Commons, it will become law in the first session of a new Parliament if the Government comes back, and the only remedy for a real anti suffragist will be to prevent the Government coming back.' He went on, however, in a more cheerful vein. 'Almost everybody believes that Home Rule will get through under the Parliament Act and probably—subject to a deal—Welsh Disestablishment. After that we shall have new politics—land etc.—and new risks, but the Unionist party is so stupid that I begin to think it can be relied upon to pull us out of any pit we may dig for ourselves.'[1]

Both militant and non-militant Suffragists were actively working to deepen the Liberal 'pit', and prevent the Unionists extracting their enemies from it. The Pankhurst organization, its suspicions amply confirmed, stepped up its 'guerrilla militancy' and invited government action. The Fawcett organization, full of high-minded resolve, moved more actively into Labour party preparations for the coming election. In a pamphlet, issued early in February, it flatly rejected the government's offer of a Private Member's bill, quoting Balfour to the effect that Unionist sympathisers had agreed in caucus to resist such a measure coming under the Parliament Act. Philip Snowden made the same point in another pamphlet, and went on 'The woman suffrage question will now dominate British politics until it is settled. It has within the last four weeks killed a great Government measure and . . . It has made it impossible for any succeeding Liberal Government to deal with franchise reform without giving votes to women. The Labour Party will see to that.'[2]

[1] Papers of Herbert, Viscount Gladstone, B.M. Add. Mss. 46042, J. A. Spender to Gladstone, 2 February 1913.
[2] Snowden, Philip, *The Dominant Issue* (Pamphlet, N.P., February 1913).

The Pankhurst campaign now began to include more and more arson, and this new element gave the government an opportunity to move beyond sentences of imprisonment, hamstrung as these were by the tactic of the hunger strike. On 11 February in the cabinet meeting there was a 'long discussion . . . in regard to the proper method of dealing with the various forms of outrages'.[3] By early March, with Mrs. Pankhurst on bail pending trial for blowing up Lloyd George's house at Walton Heath, the Home Secretary in cabinet 'submitted a draft Bill to empower the re-arrest of persons discharged because of self inflicted ill health'. Asquith noted for the King that 'Its further consideration by the Cabinet was adjourned till next week after a strong protest by Mr. Burns who thinks that no steps (beyond the provision of facilities to food and drink) should be taken to prevent prisoners . . . from starving themselves.'[4] This was the origin of the Prisoners (Temporary Discharge for Ill Health) Bill, soon to be known as the 'Cat and Mouse Act'. Introduced in late March by McKenna, it was sent to the Lords on 23 April, and went through all the stages the following day. Their Lordships—including the suffragist Haldane—saw no reason for delay. This was the immediate consequence of Liberal inability to deal with Suffrage. If coercion of militants there must be, then a way had to be sought to neutralize the hunger strike—a way short of the politically dangerous course of Mr. Burns. The system of licensing release on health grounds gave the government a reasonably effective weapon for the continuous harrying of the Pankhursts and their followers.

The other necessity was an end to Plural Voting. In mid-March, when the cabinet had authorized McKenna to proceed with his Prisoners' Release Bill, it had also considered and approved a draft of a one-clause bill prohibiting such voting. This, the sole survivor of the Franchise and Registration Bill, was a measure talked of years earlier by Gladstone and rejected by the House of Lords

[3] Papers of the Earl of Oxford and Asquith, Vol. 7, F. 13, Asquith to H.M. the King, 11 February 1913.

[4] *Ibid.*, F. 17, Asquith to H.M. the King, 6 March 1913.

in 1906. That it would need the Parliament Act for its passage was taken for granted; hence, in view of its significance to Liberal election prospects, it must needs soon be in the legislative programme. To the opposition its very introduction at this date indicated that the government did not intend an election before early 1915. Evidence that this was the case is given in a letter of Herbert Samuel to Gladstone of 16 March where he stated 'I do not see any prospect of the defeat of our Government, or of a dissolution before the spring of 1915 unless the King was to commit the incredible folly of listening to some unwise advisors and trying to force his Ministers to dissolve before Home Rule passes under the Parliament Act and, failing our acquiescence, to dismiss us.'[5]

The degree to which the Irish question was overshadowing all other considerations is quite clear in this letter. The Lords' power of delay built into the Parliament Act was forcing the political struggle not to subside, but to increase so greatly that cabinet ministers in early 1913—and certainly later—saw their task as a grim fight to keep in step with the timetable demanded by the Act and the election that must come in 1915. In this spirit, the Plural Voting Bill was hurried to its Second Reading by the 30th April and, to the satisfaction of the government, safely rejected by the Lords in the following July. Woman Suffrage had of course reared its head in the debates of both Houses—Snowden in the Commons and Lord Lytton in the Lords insisting that the bill broke Asquith's pledge to allow Parliament to rule on Suffrage in any government franchise measure.

Once more in the pre-war period, Suffrage was debated in the Commons. This was in early May when the Dickinson Bill was refused a Second Reading. The Bill sought to enfranchise women over the age of 25 on the local government qualification if single, and as wives of householders if married. It represented the all-embracing compromise. The clause enfranchising wives of householders was aimed at satisfying Labour and Liberal M.P.s who

[5] Papers of Herbert, Viscount Gladstone, B.M. Add. Mss. 45999, F. 138–139, Herbert Samuel to Gladstone, 16 March 1913.

were unwilling to allow the enfranchising of separately qualified women. The age limit of twenty-five years—suggested over a year previously by Liberal agents—was proposed in order to remove fears of a female-dominated electorate. The precedent was valuable. In 1918 it was to be followed in the Representation of the People Act which enfranchised women—at thirty and not at twenty-five years of age. In the event the 1913 scene resembled the debates before 1911. The cabinet had agreed that only Grey and Asquith should speak. Asquith's speech was a model of lucidity. Voting, he said, was a duty and a privilege, not a right. Democracy had no quarrel with . . . 'distinctions which nature has created'. He ended by declaring that only when a majority of women wanted the vote, and Parliament neglected the interests of women, could Suffrage be 'practical politics'. Unionists could be forgiven for thinking that in 1915, after an election, Asquith, if in office, might have discovered that these conditions had been fulfilled. The division saw the bill lost by 47—54, Nationalists voting with the hostile majority.

The result in the Commons was a convincing display of the fact that no progress could be made by Private Members' bills, and that no progress would be made so long as the government remained in power. The following day, the Women's Liberal Federation, in censuring the Irish for their vote on the one hand, and congratulating the government for the Home Rule Bill on the other, expressed the dilemma of Liberal women neatly enough.

Militancy continued throughout the period to the war. The Cat and Mouse Act brought no real respite to the government, since the militants took their periods of release under license as opportunities for fund-raising, recruiting, and further militancy. In late April, after the passage of the Act, the government had tried to suppress *The Suffragette* on the ground that it incited its readers to criminal acts. Proscription in advance of this kind was, to say the least, of dubious legality and protests poured in, among them the view of Bernard Shaw that McKenna 'believes himself to be the Tsar of Russia'. The myopia and exasperation over Suffrage was making the Liberal government ever more illiberal. The doubts of friends on such a score were heightened in June by the death of Emily Wilding Davison at the Derby when she tried to pull down the King's horse. Making all allowances for clearly unbalanced individuals, supporters of the government could still become more and more anxious over the next stage of agitation and the next governmental response. Some evidence of how far Christabel Pankhurst, at least, had progressed, was to hand. Circulating during 1913 was her notorious pamphlet *The Great Scourge* in which women were virtually urged to avoid the embraces of men, three-quarters of whom, she asserted, had venereal disease. Confronted with such mistaken fervour, a Liberal might reflect gloomily, what hope would any government have?

Meanwhile the National Union had quadrupled in membership since 1909 and was now organized in 411 societies all over the country. Committed to its aim of removing 'the Anti Suffrage element in the party in power' it stood ready, in 1913, to work for that end in 156 constituencies, and generally to refuse any aid to an 'official Liberal candidate'. In July it began a series of 'Pilgrimages' from all parts of the country which culminated in a huge demonstration in London and an interview with the Prime Minister on 8 August. Asquith had to listen while Mrs. Margaret Robinson noted the change in working-class attitudes to Suffrage after the publication of the accounts of the National League for Opposing Woman Suffrage. These showed, she asserted, 'that Lord Rothschild has given £3,000 and running through the gamut of dukes and lords . . . What I have found is that working men have discovered this and they are inclined to regard the opposition to Woman Suffrage as a Conservative and Liberal Plutocracy against Democracy.' When Mrs. Fawcett referred to evidence that the Irish had been ready to kill Suffrage in the Franchise Bill, at the request of ministers, Asquith broke in to deny it. In his reply to the deputation he began by agreeing that Private Member's bills were of little use. 'Under our present Parliamentary system the facilities for what are called "Private Member's Bills" are, unless the Government show them some special favour, scanty and precarious.' He then defended the Reform

Bill, 'There was not an authority whom we consulted . . . who did not agree with us, and we had precedents which seemed to be directly in point. We had the precedent of 1867 and 1884, on both of which occasions Women's Suffrage amendments were admitted, discussed, and divided on—I think in both cases it was divided on in two bills with no wider title than our own . . .' He then denied that he personally had intervened with Liberals in the Commons—'so far as I am concerned there is not one shadow of foundation for it'. Dealing with questions afterwards, he put to himself the question 'whether or not if the Liberal Government —and there are a lot of "ifs"—are then in power . . . whether it would not then be the duty of the Liberal Government, whatever might be the personal opinions of some of its members on the matter, to introduce and make themselves responsible for a Franchise Bill including Women's Suffrage?'[6] By August 1913 this was the key question for the future so far as Suffragists were concerned—and Asquith refused to answer. This reluctance to envisage what a future Liberal government would do may be pardonable. With Home Rule not yet law the King, increasingly concerned about Ulster developments, was pressing him for a General Election or, alternatively, for a conference of the parties on some general devolution of political power. Ireland was becoming Asquith's sole concern; he refused to hold an election until Home Rule was law and yet the government seemed unable, to its satisfaction, to include or exclude Ulster from the operation of the Act. All the way up to August 1914 the dilemma increased in intensity.

Meanwhile, Suffragists continued to pester and prepare for an election. A Women's Liberal Federation pamphlet of early 1914 showed where the effort was most needed. 'It is very important to get men to take up the subject in their Associations and to send resolutions to their Members of Parliament; for we shall never get it adopted as a Government measure, or even as a party measure, until it is felt to be more popular in the country as a whole. What

---

[6] Asquith Papers, Box 89, F. 47–85, Mr. Asquith's reply to the Suffrage delegation.

we must strive for is that the next Parliament shall be returned with a clear instruction from the constituencies to carry a demo-cratic measure of woman suffrage.'[7]

Some months earlier another pamphlet had asked for Suffrage 'Because the grant of the vote to women on a broad basis, includ-ing the wives of working men, would help in the struggle for all that Liberals hold most dear, such as the maintenance of Free Trade and Free Military Service, the reform of the Land Laws, the reform of Education, the raising of the standard of Temper-ance and Purity.'[8] This order of precedence is interesting if only because Temperance and Purity rank so low. Had the pamphlet been primarily for female consumption, convention would have demanded a higher priority for both campaigns. Suffragists had to face the dilemma that men, generally, were not impressed by the justice of Woman Suffrage, but did respond to the offer of future help in pressing for causes which involved them. Women might *ask* for the vote for themselves, but could *demand* it to support other causes.

In October the two chief friends of Suffrage in the cabinet both saw delegations of Suffragists. Grey on the 22nd told the Northern Men's Federation that their demand for government action amounted to a demand for the break-up of the government and that, anyway, because of the Parliament Act, there was no time. Everything, he said, depended on the next election: the withdrawal of the Franchise Bill tied Suffrage and Franchise Reform together and 'That has given the whole question an actuality which it had not had before.'[9] Lloyd George, at Oxford the following day, told a deputation, 'I think this Parliament has been ruined so far as Suffrage is concerned . . . I do not despair at all, if at the next General Election women are well organised and present their case to the electorate rationally . . . '. A month

[7] Pamphlet, *What Shall We do Next?* (Women's Liberal Federation, London, 1914).

[8] Pamphlet, *Why Must the Women's Liberal Federation Work for Women's Suffrage?* (W.L.F., London, September 1913).

[9] Pamphlet, *Deputation at Berwick to Sir Edward Grey*, 22 October 1913 (Northern Men's Federation for Woman Suffrage, 1913).

later, again at Oxford, Lloyd George returned to the same theme, and read his audience an oblique lecture on the nature of politics, and of the Liberal party.

There are two ways in which you can carry bills. One is by having a great wave of feeling behind the bill, the other is by use of the party machinery . . . You have got a majority of the Tory Party against you: you have a third of the Liberal Party against you. Therefore the only alternative is to secure a majority of the country and you have not got it . . . I am not condemning militancy, morally. I am condemning it tactically . . . I would not be prepared to say that the first militant movement did not attract attention . . . but I think you have gone too far . . . You have quarrelled with Irishmen . . . with Welshmen . . . with property . . . the Liberal Party; you have gone to Nonconformist meetings, peace meetings, temperance meetings.[10]

In December 1913 the Unionist Caucus resolved 'That it is inexpedient to grant the Parliamentary franchise to women on any terms until the great constitutional change has received the express sanction of the electors'. Philip Snowden, in an article, dwelt on Asquith's oblique offer to Mrs. Fawcett in August to the effect that if the election returned a majority of Suffrage Liberals, he would stand aside. The only hope for Suffrage, he concluded, was that it could be made an election issue, for 'it is no use expecting a Government measure in this Parliament'.[11]

The Labour party conference of January 1914 was predictably turbulent. A Women's Labour League resolution, asking the conference to endorse its opposition to a franchise bill which ignored Suffrage was passed, but not without resistance from the leaders of the Clerks and Textile workers. A Fabian resolution asking that the government's Plural Voting Bill be opposed until Suffrage was granted was, nevertheless, opposed by MacDonald, who pointed to the value of the bill for Labour as well as for

[10] 'Mr. Lloyd George at Oxford, 23 October 1913', *The Liberal Magazine*, Vol. 21, No. 242, November 1913 (Lib. Pub. Dept., London, 1914).
[11] Snowden, Philip, 'The Present Position of Woman Suffrage', *The Englishwoman*, Vol. 20, No. 60, December 1913, pp. 241–8.

Liberals. With an election approaching, delegates responded to this plea and voted the resolution down by a vote of 18 : 1.[12] The issue was a delicate one in a shaken party. Beatrice Webb might sneer that the Conference . . . 'was a personal triumph for J. R. MacDonald . . . There was much discontent among the I.L.P. delegates, but the solid phalanx of Miners and Textiles don't want the Labour members to cut loose from the Liberal Party and MacDonald knows it . . .'[13] MacDonald himself, however, had much to contend with from the Women's Labour League, as he revealed to Mrs. Bruce Glasier. '. . . This development of the woman's movement, and this capturing of our own by prepared resolutions is a very great menace. By and by we shall not be safe unless we too protect ourselves by wire pulling and night marches . . . our people feel and do not think.'[14] In the long run, MacDonald felt, Suffrage would help the Labour party. It must not be allowed to harm it in the short run.

Liberals would not have disagreed with this conclusion, though they would have claimed to have as much to hope for in the long run as Labour. One factor which is interesting from the Suffrage viewpoint is the situation revealed by Redmond in a report of an interview he had with Asquith on 2 February. The Prime Minister had clearly laid out the difficulties he foresaw. 'He thinks they will fight the Army Bill in the House of Commons, and possibly resort to extreme disorder of such a character that, probably with the connivance of the Speaker, the whole business of the House will be held up.'[15] The Speaker, it seemed to some M.P.s, had ceased to be impartial and was in alliance, albeit covertly, with extreme Unionists. Perhaps he had been so earlier

[12] Report of Fourteenth Annual Conference of the Labour Party, Glasgow, 27–9 January 1914.
[13] Cole, Margaret, Ed., *Beatrice Webb's Diaries* 1912–14 (Longman, Green and Co., London, 1952), 6 February, 1914, p. 17.
[14] Lord Elton, *The Life of J. Ramsay MacDonald* (Collins, London, 1939), MacDonald to Mrs. Bruce Glasier, 4 April 1914, p. 163.
[15] Papers of John Redmond, File—Home Rule 1914. Irish Nat. Lib. Mss. 15,165. On this see also Collin, A. M., *The Observer and J. L. Garvin 1908–14* (O.U.P. 1960), pp. 413–31.

when he had embarrassed and offended Cabinet suffragists, even perhaps the Prime Minister?

The conference between Redmond and Asquith was one of a series—it was in fact part of the prelude to the offer of limited exclusion of Ulster from the Home Rule Bill, which was made in early March in a government White Paper. Thereafter, Ireland completely absorbed the cabinet. Its attempts to prepare for unrest in Ireland, and Unionist attempts to endanger the Army Annual Act, led on 20 March to virtual mutiny at the Curragh Camp. The story of this and the subsequent gun-running episodes have no place here. It is, however, worth noting that three days after the Curragh incident, while the crisis was at its height, Grey, writing to Asquith on proposals made by Bonar Law, noted '... we should say to Bonar Law that we cannot accept his offer of a Referendum without the Plural Voter, but that we will offer him instead a General Election without the Plural Voter...'[16]

The Plural Voter had clearly assumed crucial significance in the minds of ministers—he seemed capable of defeating Home Rule by returning the Unionists, either via referendum, or general election. Little wonder the government had hastily rescued the relevant clauses from the Franchise Bill. If they could think of the Plural Voter during an Army mutiny he was clearly central to their future plans. Likewise, if he entered into the negotiations between the Prime Minister and the Leader of the Opposition at such a time, he was clearly not unimportant to the Unionists. In January 1913 when Bonar Law had prodded the Speaker into ruling he was, perhaps, at least as concerned to delay Plural Voting legislation as to emasculate Suffrage amendments. He knew, anyway, that Asquith was ready to acquiesce in the destruction of Suffrage.

Woman Suffragists, in and out of Parliament, waited for a General Election to advance their cause. Suffrage sympathizers among the Tories, too, were worried by Bonar Law's lack of

[16] Papers of Lord Grey of Falloden, Vol. 99, Grey to Asquith, 23 March 1914.

direction on the question. Lord Robert Cecil wrote to him in early June urging him not 'to drift into the same kinds of opposition on the question as have the present Ministry . . .'[17] Ireland would have to wait until the passage of the Plural Voting Bill under the Parliament Act allowed the government to call that Election. We saw earlier how the franchise question had always been entangled with the question of Irish redistribution. It is clear that during 1914 a part of the franchise question—Plural Voting—had succeeded in dangerously complicating the Irish question.

On 20 June 1914, three days before the government's bill to exclude Ulster came to the Lords, Asquith saw a deputation of the East End Federation of Suffragists. The speakers made much of the working conditions of their members. In reply the Prime Minister noted that some of the legislation of 'my administration' had improved these and cited the Trades Boards Bill and the institution of female Factory Inspectors. He recognized the Federation's separation from the militants, whose '. . . criminal methods . . . have done to much to impede the progress of your Cause . . . [and] . . . I am much more glad to hear first hand from the people who are actually concerned in it . . . than from outside advocates, however eloquent, able, and trustworthy they may be'. On Suffrage he asserted that if it was to be granted, 'you must give it to them on the same terms as men . . . If the discrimination of sex is not sufficient to justify giving the vote to one sex and the withholding of it from another, it follows *a fortiori* it seems to me that discrimination of sex does not justify . . . giving women a restricted form of franchise while you give the men an unrestricted form . . . If the change has to come, we must face it boldly and make it thoroughgoing and democratic in its basis.'[18] Here he was hinting at little less than adult suffrage. To ardent Suffragists this was totally unsatisfactory, since they felt it was hopeless to ask

[17] Papers of Andrew Bonar Law, 32/4/2, Lord Robert Cecil to Bonar Law, 4 June 1914.

[18] Asquith Papers, Box 89, F. 125–52. Deputation from the East End Federation of Suffragists, 20 June 1914.

Parliament to create an electorate having a majority of women. This view had been common in Tory circles all along. It was being repeated at this time in a memorandum of Walter Long to Bonar Law, then engaged in negotiations in Ireland with the Master of Elibank. One of the issues discussed was a small Royal Commission to examine the electoral system. 'The Franchise is in a hopeless muddle. We have one franchise for Parliament, another for the municipalities. This is costly, ridiculous, and confusing, and, incidentally, a Commission of this kind might, I believe, be able to deal with the question of woman suffrage. I am entirely opposed to the extension of the franchise to women, but as an illustration I would say that if such a Commission were to recommend a comprehensive reform of our Electoral system, with the municipality as a basis of the franchise, my objection to Women Suffrage would disappear, as we should no longer be exposed to the risk of government by women.'[19]

War seemed unlikely to change minds on the extent of any grant of Suffrage to women. It was, however, instrumental in changing minds on the principle and expediency of some grant of parliamentary representation. Asquith had certainly prepared his own escape route from his previous position—his statement to the East End Federation was, as George Dangerfield noted,[20] of some considerable significance. The Federation, and Sylvia Pankhurst particularly, may have been excluded from the WSPU but could hardly be seen as non-militant in stance. Yet it was to working-class women—militancy aside—that he chose to reveal his changing position. Such women, he knew, would support his refusal to tolerate the enfranchisement of a separately qualified 'property' vote and would realize that a 'democratic' measure would entail a battle inside the Liberal party, and certainly one between Liberals and Tories. With, seemingly, a General Election

[19] Petrie, Sir Charles, *Walter Long* (Hutchinson and Co. Ltd., London, 1936), p. 184.
[20] Dangerfield, George, *The Strange Death of Liberal England* (Paladin, London, 1966), pp. 336–8.

not too far away Asquith was firing the opening shot of the campaign.

In the event much else intervened before Asquith changed his position and he had ceased to be Prime Minister by then. The memo was received on the day of the assassination at Sarajevo. A month later, with the Buckingham Palace Conference having failed, Ireland stood on the edge of civil war and England only days away from entry into what became World War I. Edwardian England had witnessed extraordinary female militancy and perseverance. Would war divert this energy and fury into other channels and leave the feminist cause high and dry?

X.   War and Suffrage

. . . it does seem to me to be a great pity
in something quite unconnected with the
war to hit our party like this . . .
Edwin Montagu to Maurice Bonham Carter,
September 1916.

'You do the heavy truculent working man'
said D. to Henderson, 'and then I will do my
bit.'
Lloyd George to Arthur Henderson,
March 1917.

The 'terrible ifs' had accumulated and the country was at war.
Few thought it would or could last very long, or envisaged the
totality of mobilization, sacrifice and effort that it would call for.
In the outburst of patriotism and bellicosity witnessed in the first
weeks, few could be found who would guess how near the country
could come to defeat and ruin.

For politicians war changed the stakes of politics. At first there
was the formal freezing of political debate as it existed. Consideration of the Irish and Welsh Church Bills was suspended and a
political truce was concluded between the parties. By-elections
would not be contested—the relative strengths in the Commons
would remain the same. The truce, however, did not lessen the
friction between ministers, or that between the government and
the opposition. For Suffragists the war posed an immediate question, namely, what attitude they should take towards it? Mrs.
Pankhurst, a Germanophobe since her days in Paris in 1870,
made Belgium the touchstone of her attitude. McKenna released
Suffragette prisoners, and on 13 August a proclamation suspen-

ded the activities of the Women's Social and Political Union with the words ' . . . we believe that under the joint rule of enfranchised women and men the nations of the world will, owing to women's influence and authority, find a way of reconciling the claims of peace and honour, and of regulating international relations without bloodshed . . . we ardently desire that our country shall be victorious—this because we hold that the existence of small nationalities is at stake, and that the status of France and Great Britain is involved . . . It will be the future task of women, and only they can perform it, to ensure that the present world tragedy . . . shall not be repeated.'[1]

For Mrs. Fawcett's National Union the problem proved more difficult—its democratic constitution prevented dictation of attitudes by its leaders. On 4 August 1914, Mrs. Fawcett had signed the Appeal for Peace of the International Woman Suffrage Association then meeting in London. Lord Robert Cecil hastened to write regretting this step, 'Even to me the action seems so unreasonable under the circumstances as to shake my belief in the future of women to deal with great Imperial questions.'[2] Before this had reached Mrs. Fawcett she had, in a message to her members, declared, 'Women, your country needs you. As long as there was any hope for peace, most members of the National Union probably sought for peace, and endeavoured to support those who were trying to maintain it. But we have another duty now . . . Let us show ourselves worthy of citizenship, whether our right to it be recognised or not.'[3]

Patriotism and expedient politics came together neatly—the very necessary contribution to any war effort could build an overwhelming case for Suffrage. Mrs. Fawcett never ceased to hold this view. She had, however, to defend it, and from the outset at that. Many on her executive committee and among the

[1] Papers of Mrs. E. Pankhurst, Folder—Demonstrations and Political Action. Circular from Mrs. Pankhurst, 13 August 1914.
[2] Papers of Mrs. M. G. Fawcett, Vol. 4, Woman Suffrage 1913–16, Lord Robert Cecil to Mrs. Fawcett, 5 August 1914.
[3] Strachey, Ray, *Millicent Garret Fawcett* (John Murray, London, 1931), p. 276.

rank and file of the National opposed support for the war effort.
Feminists the world over, appalled by the conflict, sought means
to ameliorate and end it. In December 1914, when a proposal for
a Women's Peace Conference at The Hague lay before her, Mrs.
Fawcett wrote to the President of the International Woman Suffrage Association. 'I am very strongly opposed to your calling any
international convention, mainly for the reason that women are
as subject as men are to national prepossessions and susceptibili-
ties, and it would hardly be possible to bring together the women
of the belligerent countries without violent bursts of anger . . . I
feel *so* strongly against the proposed convention that I would
decline to attend it, and, if necessary, would resign my office in
the International Woman Suffrage Association if it were judged
incumbent on me in that capacity to take part in the Convention.'[4] In February 1915, the National Union's Council met for
the first time under war conditions. Aware that the majority of
her officers were not with her, Mrs. Fawcett openly challenged
their position by declaring that, until German troops were out of
France and Belgium, 'I believe it is akin to treason to talk of
peace.'[5] This could not be ignored and in March all the officers
(save Mrs. Fawcett and the Treasurer) and ten of the Executive
Committee resigned in protest. Mrs. Fawcett now had charge of
the National Union and, in Birmingham in June, her stand was
vindicated. Her biographer later noted 'The silent, inarticulate
voters, and the smaller societies were unanimously with her, and
the pacifists, eloquent, devoted and beloved as they were, had but
an individual following in some of the big towns.'[6] Mrs. Fawcett
had called the old world in to redress the balance of the new.

The National Union shed its pacifist wing and was thereafter
free to contribute to the war effort. The Pankhurst organization
had smaller problems with its pacifists and became bellicose in
tone. An announcement of 4 October 1915 heralded the amalgam-
ation of *The Suffragette* into *The Britannia*—an act performed
'in the name of the British Women's equality of political right
and duty, and also as a pledge of devotion to the nation of which

[4] *Ibid.*, pp. 283–4.   [5] *Ibid.*, p. 289.   [6] *Ibid.*, p. 295.

we are privileged to be members'.[7] Times had changed for the Pankhursts—though Sylvia Pankhurst, expelled from the main organization in 1913, remained hostile to the war.

In the cabinet, too, events were afoot which promised a revival of the franchise question. The Parliament Act, unless amended, called for the election of a new Parliament after 1915. The task of revising the register was due to begin, as usual, in April. The question was whether or not to continue the process with millions of men away from their homes. Further, the Plural Voting Bill which had passed the Commons in 1913 and 1914 lacked the third passage which would allow it—assuming a third rejection by the Lords—to come into force via the Parliament Act. These questions forced the cabinet to consider electoral and franchise questions and those in turn brought up Women Suffrage.

In May the government became a coalition, Churchill in disgrace removed from the Admiralty to the Duchy of Lancaster, Haldane being forced to resign and Bonar Law, Balfour, and Arthur Henderson joining the cabinet. This offered not only wartime unity, but also the prospect of some all-party agreement on contentious franchise and electoral questions. Evidence to the contrary on both counts was quickly forthcoming. By mid-June a bill to amend the Parliament Act and postpone local government elections was being drafted. By July a bill existed which proposed in addition the creation of 'special registers' to replace the dated, extant register. Part of the dispute in cabinet over this related to the Plural Voter. A Cabinet Committee report of 12 November, noting the missing third passage of the Plural Voter Act, rejected 'any idea of introducing this controversial question into the House of Commons during the war . . . ' and asked Liberal leaders to 'urge this course on their followers'. It went on to argue that the five-year Parliaments envisaged in the Parliament Act were meant to be 'five peaceful years' and in this sense the Parliament elected in December 1910 could continue for one year and four months after the war had ended. During that period any bill passing could

[7] Fawcett Papers, *ibid.*, Mrs. Pankhurst to Mrs. Badley, 4 October 1915.

be reckoned 'as having been passed in a session immediately successive to the session of 1914'. Here then was a proposal for automatic extension of the life of Parliament and for the subsequent election to be fought *without* the Plural Voter. In the event the suggestion was not accepted and the Registration Act of 1915 kept the old register as valid for the year that Parliament was extended. Since by this Act the problem was deferred, not resolved another Act in early 1916 had to be passed to keep the register valid until Parliament 'directed otherwise'. To a cabinet deeply embroiled over the direction of the war and the need fully to organize for it—the question of conscription—there could be little agreement on such matters.

A cabinet paper from the Local Government Board on 9 March 1916 set out the problems succinctly.[8] There was need, it argued, for 'a comprehensive Bill simplifying our present system of franchise and registration which is a disgrace to any civilised country'. The existence of a coalition, it went on, offered a good chance to secure agreement for a simple residential qualification a continuous registration system and equitable redistribution There were, of course, certain practical difficulties 'In the first place, it is doubtful whether any simplification of franchise would be allowed unless the question of female suffrage was settled.' As in 1912, it was precisely this ingredient which deepened cabinet disagreement, especially when seen in the context of pressure for Adult Suffrage. On 12 May Arthur Henderson circulated a paper on 'Necessary Electoral Changes', in which he stressed Adult Suffrage as the only 'final settlement' which would 'reconcile them [the working classes] to the inevitable hardships of universal compulsion . . .' and prevent politicians wasting time and energy on franchise matters 'out of all proportion to their real consequence . . . ' As for Woman Suffrage and the fear of a female majority in the electorate, he claimed, this could 'be met by making twenty-five the age at which the suffrage could be exercised in the case of women . . . '. This he asserted would be 'acceptable to the women's organisations'.

[8] Cabinet Document XIV (2), 9 March 1916.

Outside cabinet, Suffragists and their allies watched with anxiety. In January W. H. Dickinson, a prominent Liberal Suffragist, had written to Mrs. Fawcett urging her to ask that the cabinet resolve the Suffrage dilemma by setting up a Speakers' Conference. By May, primed by Henderson and Lord Robert Cecil, Mrs. Fawcett wrote to ask Asquith to declare his intentions. The Prime Minister replied that if there were to be legislation 'the considerations set out in your letter will be fully weighed without any prejudgement from the controversies of the past'.

The cabinet was deadlocked on both the question of general franchise reform and Suffrage. As May ended Asquith reported to the King that the cabinet was debating 'the expediency of providing some form of Registration which would enable an election to be held on the expiry of the present Parliament. It was agreed that no such machinery could be devised in time to be operative by the date at which, under existing legislation, this Parliament comes to an end. There was, however, much difference of opinion as to the practicability of forming a register (to include soldiers and sailors) for the year 1917. In the end a Cabinet Committee was instructed to consider the various aspects of the matter.' The Committee, consisting of Samuel, Bonar Law, Harcourt, Lloyd George, Henderson, Wood and the Attorney-General, made little progress and in July its failure was confessed when, as Asquith noted to the King, 'it was decided to ask the House of Commons, whom the subject peculiarly concerns, to set up a Select Committee to consider it'.

In the Commons Asquith seemed at first able to control the swelling opposition. A few days later on 19 July a statement by Samuel, stressing only the difficulties and the degree of cabinet deadlock involved, caused uproar; the House refused the requested Select Committee. The problem was thus returned to the cabinet. For over three further weeks the cabinet twisted and turned in disagreement about both the 'soldier vote' and the principle of Woman Suffrage. On 26 July, principal Liberal agents had gathered in London to discuss the various problems. Gulland the Chief Whip, reporting to Walter Runciman, noted that ' . . . the trend of public opinion is now in favour of granting . . . the franchise to soldiers, sailors, munitions workers and women. The change of public opinion in respect of the extension of the franchise to women is very marked.'[9] Evidence of this nature could not break the deadlock. Not until three further proposals—none of which mentioned Suffrage—were turned down by the Commons did Asquith and Walter Long succumb to the inevitable. Introducing yet another proposal on 14 August, Asquith made public his conversion to the principle of Suffrage and a few days later Walter Long, shortly before Parliament adjourned, followed suit. Both parties now appeared to be committed to some measure and this, in itself, closed a chapter of political history.

Principle was one thing, legislation quite another. All the old bogeys were resurrected as full of life, seemingly, as they had ever been. Walter Long seemed to be setting the pace. First in a letter and then in a memorandum of 23 August, he circulated to the cabinet ideas on the subject of a Registration Conference. This would discuss all the explosive issues resulting from reform of registration and franchise and redistribution of seats. He suggested that an ex-judge be Chairman and that the Conference should seek 'The adoption of a system under which fair consideration would be given to the representation of interests rather than mere numbers . . . Many think . . . there ought to be proportional representation.'[10]

Much hung on 'mere numbers' in the country at large and in France at that very moment and, not least, on *who* constituted the numbers at any conference. Membership would be the first and vital battle to influence the context of the post-war electoral scene. Hence the issues at stake were very large indeed, potentially. The pre-war scene had been seriously affected by left-over franchise business—registration and qualification, including Suffrage. Here now was an opportunity to find honourable ways out of

[9] Papers of Walter Runciman, WR 141, Gulland to Runciman, 27 July 1916.
[10] Papers of the Earl of Oxford and Asquith, Vol. 17, Misc. Letters, July–December 1917, F. 48, Walter Long to Asquith, 18 August 1916.

some dilemmas, certainly—but not at the expense of prejudging post-war politics.

The whole story of the infighting over Conference membership is now somewhat obscured. Deciding who would attend the Conference merely aggravated the struggle. On 8 September, Long circulated a list of would-be members and noted 'It is believed that there is a preponderance of Anti Suffragists, which would appear to be right in view of the magnitude of the issues involved in the adoption of a reform which has never yet been sanctioned even in abstract form by Parliament.' Three days later Edwin Montagu—a supposed ally of Asquith—replied in a tart letter. He rejected the idea that only M.P.s could be members of the Conference, and the notion that a Peer be Chairman. He went on—'I dissent from the view that the Conservative Party should obtain an extra representative who is to be called a Unionist representative. It is a novel ideal to me that the Ulster members are a separate party acting separately from the rest of the Conservative Party. I dissent emphatically from the suggestion that the Conference should be weighted against Women's Suffrage.'[11]

Long replied the following day. Asquith, he claimed, had approved of keeping the Conference within Parliament, and of the idea of a Peer as Chairman. On the question of university representation he noted, a trifle ingenuously, that 'There is no idea of politics in the suggestion that there should be a University representative. The idea was solely to secure that the questions should be considered from the University point of view.' On the Ulster Unionist members he was hardly more subtle 'I think', he wrote, 'you are rather mistaken in your criticism. The point is that Irish Franchise questions differ materially from the British and, in securing consideration of these, it is not unreasonable that all three Parties in Ireland should be represented.'[12]

Montagu was much less than satisfied. He asked Maurice Bonham Carter to check if Asquith had indeed approved. He commented, 'The House of Lords has nothing to do with Franchise,

[11] *Ibid.*, F. 81, Edwin Montagu to Walter Long, 11 September 1916.
[12] *Ibid.*, F. 83, Walter Long to Montagu, 12 September 1916.

it does not vote, and I think it is a monstrous thing to have a Peer in the Chair.' He went on revealingly—'Whatever be the idea underlying the University representative and the Irish Franchise question, the fact remains that as a result there are 10 Conservatives to 8 Liberals. After all, there is the future to think of and it does seem to me to be a great pity in something quite unconnected with the War to hit our party like this. If the University question ought to be represented, and if the Ulster Unionists are Unionists and not a separate party, then why not see that in your 8 Conservatives, one is a University man and one is an Irishman? I still think it is grossly unfair to weight the Conference against Women's Suffrage. The least you could do in the present state of public opinion is to have both sides represented equally.'[13]

Walter Long, meanwhile, was writing to Asquith to comment on the criticisms of his suggestions made by Mr. Gulland of the Scottish Liberal Whip's Office. The Peers, he claimed, must be represented if the reform of the Lords was to appear non-controversial. On the composition of the Conference he noted—'If the representatives of the Liberal Party, the Irish Party, and the Labour Party are taken together . . . there is a clear majority over all the Unionists; and my own opinion is . . . that there is much more likely to be forcible objection on this score than upon any other. On all these questions—Franchise, Registration, Re-distribution—there is, so far as I know, no difference of opinion between Liberals, Irish and Labour, and I myself should find it very difficult to support a proposal which put the Unionist Party, not only in a minority upon the whole Conference, but in a minority greatly increased by the fact that there would be a combination against them by the three Parties. I believe that numbers are fair. I had no thought of party politics in selecting the names . . . Of course it will not rest with me to decide what our attitude is to be, but I cannot believe that Lord Lansdowne and Mr. Bonar Law would consent to what I understand to be Mr. Gulland's proposals.' He ended with a frank avowal of his motives in suggesting the Conference method of solution. 'If we cannot

[13] *Ibid.*, F. 80–1, Montagu to M. Bonham Carter, 13 September 1916.

get these thorny questions considered and decided by a conference of some sort, we shall have to go on with our Bill, and shall be met immediately by a motion of Sir Edward Carson to enfranchise soldiers and sailors, and by another, proposed by Sir John Simon, to enfranchise women. These two will open the door to a whole-sale reform of the franchise and may easily lead us into an extremely difficult position . . .'[14]

Here was a clear plea to both leaderships to prevent the running being made by zealots of many shades in both parties. On such explosive questions, as Long frankly admitted, it was vital that there should be co-operation between, and leadership from, the front benches. Anything less would lead easily to a reversion to the arid pre-war position of stalemate and rancour. In addition, given the expectant state of public opinion, as Montagu had earlier noted, it was clear that the 'killing' of Suffrage by any method would lead to a dangerous reversion to massive dissatisfaction among thousands of women whom publicly politicians were praising for their war efforts.

Agreement of sorts followed and, by 1 October, the Speaker was writing to accept the Chairmanship though 'it will be almost impossible to attain anything approaching unanimity upon the more important topics which will come up for discussion'.[15] The Conference opened on 12 October and met regularly thereafter. While it did so, however, Carson on the soldier vote question, and Simon on Suffrage, kept up a running battle with the government. On 1 November the cabinet—despite the existence of the Conference—agreed that 'if a possible machinery can be devised, soldiers and sailors serving abroad, and otherwise qualified, ought to be able to cast their votes. The scheme for proxy voting, favoured by Mr. Long, was referred to a small Cabinet Committee for consideration.'[16] No mention here of Suffrage. The same night, in the House, Carson provoked uproar during

[14] *Ibid.*, F. 85–6, Walter Long to Asquith, 17 September 1916.
[15] *Ibid.*, F. 93, The Speaker to Asquith, 1 October 1916.
[16] *Ibid.*, Vol. 8, Cabinet Letters 1915–16, F. 207, Asquith to H.M. the King, 1 November 1916.

the Committee Stage of the Registration Bill. Herbert Samuel, reporting to the King, noted that 'In the course of the discussion the crux of the difficulty was not raised, namely that if the franchise is extended to soldiers, sailors as such, the advocates of Woman Suffrage will insist that their claims be considered.'[17] Long wrote to Asquith 'In my judgement unless some big stroke is made next week, the Government will be in serious danger . . . it seems to me that the only course open is to jump the House of Commons at its decision last night . . . I would suggest a motion enfranchising soldiers, sailors and munition workers over 21; the motion to be moved by Carson . . . If the House comes to a decision on the question the Government should proceed on the lines of the decision.'[18]

This suggestion was disregarded, and on 12 November 1916 the last government Registration Bill was withdrawn when the Speaker ruled all widening amendments out of order, and support for it melted away. Carson, however, had a motion in his own name and now pressed for a bill. Writing to Asquith on 15 November, he rejected Asquith's offer of a day for discussion, saying this 'would be of very little use as amendments would be so raised that we would never get a vote upon the question in which I am interested'.[19] The strain created in the cabinet by this move by Carson was soon apparent. On 22 November Henderson and Robert Cecil in a joint letter to the Prime Minister noted 'We write to point out to you that we should be put in a very difficult position if Carson is allowed to bring the soldiers vote before the House in such a form as will preclude the discussion of women's suffrage.'[20] Such was the position when, on 9 December, Asquith resigned and Lloyd George became Prime Minister.

In 1908 the accident of health had deprived Suffragists of a

[17] Papers of Herbert, Viscount Samuel. A 52. Reports to H.M. the King, 1 November 1916.

[18] Asquith Papers, Vol. 17, Misc. Letters, July–December 1916, F. 132, Walter Long to Asquith, 2 November 1916.

[19] *Ibid.*, F. 149, Carson to Asquith, 15 November 1916.

[20] *Ibid.*, F. 155, A. Henderson and Lord Robert Cecil to Asquith, 22 November 1916.

sympathetic Prime Minister. Eight years later the fortunes of war put in to office a man committed to the expediency and political utility of Suffrage, if not fervent in his attachment to notions of justice for women. Between 1908 and 1914 the hostility of a Prime Minister, given party divisions, had proved a decisive obstacle. Those party divisions still persisted, war or no. Could a friendly Liberal leading a coalition cabinet produce a bill which would allay the fears and satisfy the hopes of enough M.P.s to prevent Suffrage once more being left aside as too contentious, too divisive?

Lloyd George indicated that he wished the Conference to continue. Further, he ensured that the two new members appointed by the Speaker, Mrs. Fouche and Lord Wortley, were both sympathetic to Suffrage and thus increased the Suffrage majority. On 22 December, Northcliffe wrote to Lady Betty Balfour asking for agitation on the Suffrage question. Five days later, writing to Mrs. Fawcett, he claimed that Lloyd George was 'very keen on the subject, and very practical too'. The same day Mrs. Fawcett, writing to Lloyd George in the belief that the corner had been turned, could be fulsome. 'We know that you are our friend as no previous Prime Minister has ever been, and we feel that you have the power to show your friendship as never before.'[21]

The Report of the Speaker's Conference was dated 27 January 1917, and was issued a few days later. It recommended basing the parliamentary franchise for men on residence and not occupation, adopting proportional representation, and simplifying the local government register. On Suffrage the Speaker noted in a preface to the Report that '. . . I endeavoured to obtain an equal division of opinion so far as it could be ascertained, but many difficulties presented themselves in discovering the views of gentlemen upon that important topic.'[22] Nevertheless, by a majority, the Conference Report recommended a grant of the franchise to qualified

[21] Fawcett Papers, Vol. 4, Mrs. Fawcett to Lloyd George, 27 December 1916.

[22] Asquith Papers, Box 32, F. 192. Report of the Speaker's Conference, 27 January 1916.

local government electors and wives of the same. It also accepted the notion of raising the qualifying age for women—thus calming fears of a female-dominated electorate and offering a sop to the Antis. The estimated increase had been 2 million men, giving a total of 10 million, and a grant of the vote to between six and seven million women. In fact the 1918 register, when revised, showed 12,913,160 men and 8,479,156 women.

On 29 March, Lloyd George saw a huge deputation of women's organizations organized by Mrs. Fawcett. The previous day Asquith had introduced a resolution calling for a prompt bill on the lines of the Speaker's Conference Report. This had been accepted by a vote of 341 to 62. The deputation therefore seemed almost superfluous, though it was known there had been a battle in cabinet. As Lloyd George's Secretary, Frances Stevenson, put it some days later in her Diary 'He (L.G.) had a tough fight in the cabinet to get the thing through as it deals a blow at the Tories. But he and Henderson arranged things between them . . . "You do the heavy truculent working man," said D. to Henderson "and then I will do my bit . . ."'[23]

The Prime Minister said that the bill would not be a government bill but a House of Commons bill, and would be drafted to include Suffrage from the outset. The age limit would be set at thirty since nothing lower, he said, would be accepted by the Commons, though such a limit effectively excluded a majority of women war workers. The same day as these assurances were given, Walter Long was writing to his brother to defend the age limit in truly conservative terms. . . . 'I think it fair to say that no agitation for an extension of the franchise to women would have any chance of success which was not accompanied by a similar demand for men, and therefore the teaching of history surely points in the direction that, if we are able to pass an agreed measure now, we may well look forward to at least another 20 or 30 years before any further change is likely to be made.'[24]

[23] A. J. P. Taylor, *Ed.*, *Lloyd George. A Diary. Frances Stevenson* (Hutchinson, London, 1971), p. 148.

[24] Petrie, Sir Charles, *Walter Long* (Hutchinson, London, 1936), p. 210.

If, however, the bill gave Long cause for satisfaction, and was supported by a majority of both major parties, the Irish Nationalists under Redmond harboured many fears. With Home Rule in abeyance, the bill would apply to Ireland, as would its corollary the Redistribution Bill, in process of being drawn up. On both counts the Nationalists stood to lose. Extension of the franchise would hasten the menacing rise of Sinn Fein, while a redistribution put through by the Commons would almost certainly favour the Unionists in Ulster thus strengthening secession demands after the war. Thus, while the Franchise Bill of 1917 was steamrollered through its stages by great majorities, the Nationalists were slowly crushed between the devil of Sinn Fein and the deep sea of Ulster machinations inside the Unionist party. Poetic justice, Suffragists might have felt.

Glimpses of this plight may be seen in the correspondence of the Nationalist dissident Tim Healy. He, if he is to be believed, spent 1917 exposing and blocking Redmondite efforts to break out from the trap. Thus on 15 May, Healy confided to his nephew Maurice 'I was afraid that the Franchise Bill was not going to be applied to Ireland, but understand it will be. There must have been some doubt about it, as the Redmondites are hostile to an extended franchise.'[25] Again to his nephew, he noted on 3 June how the Redmondites abstained from voting for the Franchise Bill, though they were all present. The bitterness of the split in Ireland among the Nationalists may be seen in the exchange between Healy and another dissident, William O'Brien. On 26 September, O'Brien wrote to Healy in gleeful anticipation of the destruction of the Redmondites. 'The one thing that matters now is to block the "Party's" plan for forcing elections before the new Franchise Bill is law. Letters like the enclosed show that, even on the existing Register, "the Party" would come back in fragments from the electors, but with the new franchise, hardly half a dozen of them could survive.'[26] The Ulster position was laid out by

[25] Healy, T. M., *Letters and Leaders of My Day* (Thornton Butterworth and Co. Ltd., London, 1928). 2 Vols., Vol. 2, p. 583.
[26] The Papers of William O'Brien, Irish National Library, Mss. 8556, O'Brien to T. Healy, 26 September 1917.

Healy in a letter of 12 October. He feared that the election would give Carson absolute control in Ulster. 'A Dissolution on present Register would mean that 20 Tories to 15 H. Rulers would be returned for Ulster. I fear the Redmondites want this to justify them for last year's Partition Policy. How Carson would rejoice in a situation which gave him 22 or 23 supporters, an absentee Shin party of 50, and a broken tail of Redmondites helpless and discredited. Finis Home Rule Act. I feel sure Lloyd George is being urged by Carson to dissolve, and the formation of the new English Party may supply the pretext. After such a General Election it would be easy to exclude Ireland from the Franchise Bill.'[27]

Redistribution, clearly, was the key to Nationalist and Ulster attitudes toward the bill. The issue which had dogged the franchise question in general and Suffrage in particular since 1885 was once more of some importance. This time, however, with both major parties resolved on a Franchise Bill, the Irish far from calling the tune, were being forced to dance—and pay the piper. In October 1917 the matter was referred to the Irish Boundary Commission under the guidance of the Speaker. When its report was delivered it had to be withdrawn in the face of determined Nationalist opposition. The matter was referred to a joint committee of Nationalists and Ulstermen, again under the Speaker. This was sitting as the Franchise Bill itself came up before the Lords in January 1918. The Nationalists were forced to accept a government-imposed redistribution in Ulster giving the Unionists control, and nothing then could save them from their destruction at the hands of the electors in December of that year. The franchise question, so long the captive of the Irish, ended by helping to destroy the last chance of a peaceful settlement in Ireland.

In November 1917 the Suffragists had been able to muster enough power to force the government to apply to local government the same qualifications for women as they proposd to apply to the parliamentary register. In December the Lords had given the bill an unopposed Second Reading. It was understood that the

[27] *Ibid.*, T. Healy to O'Brien, 12 October 1917.

opposition was saving itself for the Committee Stage due to begin on 8 January. The attitude of Curzon was unknown to Suffragists at this time—Lloyd George had said that it was to save his face in cabinet that the bill had not been made a government bill. Curzon's subsequent speech—as a leading Anti—can be seen only as the *quid pro quo* for this concession. Not until the third day of debate did Curzon speak. Then, conceding nothing on the intrinsic merit of Suffrage, he proceeded to rationalize a change of front. He concentrated on the effect of a Lords' rejection on the government and on the subject of Lords reform: '. . . your Lordships . . . can cut this clause right out of the Bill . . . but if you think that by killing the clause you can also save the Bill, I believe you to be mistaken . . . [for] . . . the House of Commons will return the Bill to you with the clause reinserted . . . if you do not give way, are you prepared to embark on a conflict with a majority of 350 in the House of Commons, of whom nearly 150 belong to the Party to which most of your Lordships also belong?'[28] The question, of course, could only have one answer, and their Lordships duly passed the clause by 134 to 71. Even had Curzon and his twelve known supporters voted against it the gesture would have availed them nothing. Suffrage passed the Lords with the Antis unable to stop it, and the leading Antis did not even join the minority in defeat.

The vote marked the end of real resistance to Woman Suffrage. The issue had inevitably become involved with the Irish question and with the curbing of the Lords. It had, too, never been a party measure and this fact had kept it from the Statute Book. Once, however, under conditions of war, a majority of the major parties acting in concert had taken it up then its passage was speedy. In that passage the Irish had no say—and no protection—and the Lords stood naked and impotent before the sweeping majorities of the Coalition.

If the impact of war on party politics and necessities was the principal cause of Suffrage success in 1918, it is as well to note

[28] Fawcett, M. G., *The Women's Victory and After* (Sidgwick and Jackson Ltd., London 1920), p. 147.

149

that Woman Suffragists had brought their issue to the point where it became one of those necessities. The threat of renewed militancy—even during the war—was not to be dismissed lightly. More positively, the task of post-war reconstruction seemed to call for settlement of the question. *The Times*, in urging the Lords to accept the Reform Bill, stressed, not the fear of renewed agitation or the rewarding of women for their efforts, but the 'injustice of withholding such protection as the vote affords from a sex which has, for the first time, taken its full share in the national effort, and will have sufficient difficulty in any case to maintain the position which it has won'.[29]

[29] *The Times*, 10 January 1918.

XI. Conclusion

The essential difficulty of the position is the division of the parties on the question. The usual political machine 'tin plating' won't work.
Herbert Gladstone to Sir Edward Grey, October 1909.

WOMAN SUFFRAGE AND BRITISH POLITICS

Woman Suffrage, whatever it was to feminists and their allies, became to the Liberal cabinet a part of the left-over franchise business of the nineteenth century. It followed, therefore, that after 1906 it was caught up in political conflict of the first magnitude. No real understanding of the campaign is possible if it is not seen in this context. A scenario which had Mrs. Pankhurst and the Prime Minister engaged in a battle of wills, with justice on one side and male obduracy on the other, may make good material for polemics, but is hardly satisfactory as a guide either to what went on, or to what both contestants thought was going on.

Woman Suffrage as a cause and an embarrassment amazed all politicians—friend and foe—by the speed with which it developed from a matter for salons and tea parties to brawls between women and policemen in Parliament Square and Downing Street. The combination of the cheap press and the dramatic new tactics of Mrs. Pankhurst and her followers meant that, within months of taking office, Liberals found themselves being assailed by the totally unforeseen. A full understanding of the impasse between the Liberal government and Suffragists must bear in mind the part played by surprise, a hasty reaction and, thereafter, an elevating of that reaction into a fixed position. No one, after all, foresaw in 1906 how far the militants would go, and how many women would follow them there. Had Asquith done so it is very likely that prudence and expediency would have dictated greater caution in taking up a position; more avenues of retreat established from it; and far less explicit and implicit support offered to people such as Loreburn and Harcourt.

In the expectations aroused by the prospect of a Liberal government, it was natural that the hopes of Suffragists would be heightened and that these would be disappointed by the campaign and its immediate aftermath. When, as for the Pankhursts, this disappointment was accompanied by ministerial evasion and by rough handling of women hecklers being tolerated by crowd and speaker then it is, perhaps, not surprising that the smouldering embers of personal and sexual resentment were quickly fanned into a blaze of rebellion and fury. The expectations aroused among workers by the appearance of the Labour Representation Committee M.P.s in 1906, and the subsequent dashing of their hopes, helped breed after 1910 a fury and despair which some Tories feared threatened the state itself. Woman Suffrage was not in this first class of issues, but it quite quickly became a first-class irritant and a cross for all politicians, and especially ministers, to bear.

The constitutional situation, as seen by the Liberal government after 1906, directly contributed to the impasse. The Lords must pass any Suffrage bill and were likely, either to reject it on principle, or to express a willingness to accept a bill which was unacceptable to a Liberal cabinet or party in Parliament. Not, as we have seen, until the Parliament Act became law was Suffrage even a remote legislative possibility. Even then the shortening of Parliament's life, and the heavy load of legislation, meant that the passage of the Franchise and Registration Bill would have been fraught with risk without, and certainly with, Suffrage clauses. Again, after 1910, the position of the Irish Nationalists was clearly crucial. By *seeming* to be the chief prop of continued Liberal government they gave the Tories a reason to oppose the government: that reason was the lack of an English majority;

which, carried to extremes, set the stage for the Curragh incident. Prior to that it is very likely that the Irish would have joined the Tories and Liberal Anti Suffragists in killing the Suffrage clauses to prevent the desperate embarrassment of Asquith. The obstacles to Suffrage were, then, formidable even had some kind of Liberal or bipartisan consensus emerged in 1912.

The party and parliamentary system made difficult the arrival at some kind of Liberal consensus inside Parliament. Those opposed to Woman Suffrage derived considerable support from the strong opposition of Asquith, Loreburn and Harcourt. Not only did such support mean that the Whip's office provided steady discouragement to ardent Suffragist Liberals, and the latent threat of official Downing Street displeasure, but, in a party out of power for a decade, there were plenty of 'hopefuls' for office who could be cajoled into silence, if not agreement. Added to this, however, there was a contrary case, before and after 1910, which Liberal Suffragists had to answer if only to maintain the legitimacy of their pressure for action by their party.

To begin with, there was the argument over principle. Asquith himself was adamant that there was no evidence that women wanted or needed the parliamentary vote. Democracy, as he said repeatedly, had no quarrel with the distinctions created by Nature. It was not good enough for his fellow Liberals to point out that virtually every organized body of women, via their own policy-making procedures, had gone on record to the contrary. Against this, as opposed to Suffrage organizations proper, Asquith used the argument of their untypicality, and of the unrepresentative nature of their leaderships. Though he made little of it publicly, it is clear that, privately, he argued that militancy on the Pankhurst model showed not a desire for political participation but proof of unfitness to participate and proof, too, of a hunger for notoriety on the part of some leaders which cast doubt upon their sanity. It is significant that the only time prior to the war that Asquith gave public notice of a potential change of position was in June 1914, when he spoke to Sylvia Pankhurst's East End Federation of Suffragists. Facing a body of working-class women led by a Pankhurst who had been expelled from the WSPU, his tone was noticeably conciliatory. His administration had helped such women, he claimed, and he was glad they now had no truck with the WSPU. He had always argued that if Suffrage were to be granted it should be in a broad democratic measure, and not some limited enfranchisement. In effect, while continuing to hold that the mass of women still might not *want* the vote, his tone indicated that he was coming to see that millions of them *needed* it.

While approaching this position, however, he had used with effect two other sets of arguments. The first was something of a subscription to the doctrine of the mandate. After 1906 he argued that Suffrage had not been put to the country at the election. By this he meant that while, as was true, 80 per cent of Liberals had given private pledges, Liberal leaders had not spoken for Suffrage or been identified in the public mind with the idea. It followed, for him, that it would be illegitimate for the government to proceed even had they been agreed. Thus, for Asquith it was illegitimate for Liberal members to press the cabinet to act—private pledges were personal opinions and not binding on the leadership. Even viewed *en masse* such pledges could not be construed as a bid to make party policy, unless the members concerned were prepared to remake party leadership—and of that there was no evidence. Even after the two elections of 1910 Asquith could argue —albeit less strongly—that the question still had not been put to the electorate, the Budget in the first election, and the Lords in the second, overshadowing all.

Put together the two arguments could not easily be dismissed. When added to the question of the *kind* of bill to be proposed, the case seemed altogether stronger. As we have seen, the eventual grant in 1918—minus the age limit of thirty—was probably the proposal commanding the widest Liberal and certainly Labour support. If after 1906 proponents of Suffrage fell to discussing bills, not principles or mandates, then certain considerations became apparent at once. Firstly it would be difficult to coerce hostile Liberals into accepting such a bill and many Liberals

would accept no less—a government bill was, therefore, somewhat unlikely. If one was going to have a Private Member's Bill
and government time for it, then it was far from certain that
enough Tories and Irish Nationalists would offset Liberal opponents. On top of this, after 1906, would the Lords accept either
bill—assuming one could be secured? The answer was, of course,
almost certainly not. Further, by precedent, an enfranchising bill
should come near the end of a parliament so that dissolution
could follow the coming into force of the new register. Assuming
a Lords rejection, would the defeat of Suffrage be an electorally
acceptable *casus belli* to confront the Lords? Again, the answer
was no. Even after the Parliament Act, as we have seen, the preparations for the Franchise and Registration Bill had to bear in
mind the imponderables of parliamentary timetables and the
reaction of the Lords whether a Suffrage clause was, or was not,
included.

Such were the arguments which were deployed. Ultimately,
of course, it was political force which triumphed in the changed
circumstances of the war. Before 1916, however, this force op-
erated to reinforce Asquith's position and give greater standing to
these arguments. The Woman Suffrage campaign was, after all, a
second-class question despite the public embarrassment and intense private indignation. Only for brief periods in 1912–13 and
1914 did it look like forcing the cabinet to consider it with
the knowledge that, inexpediently handled, the question could
threaten the unity, and hence the continuance of the Asquith
administration. The force which the question could muster lay,
not only in its intrinsic qualities, but in the fact that after 1911
and the Parliament Act it was difficult, if not impossible, to bring
up necessary suffrage business—registration questions, the Plural
Voter, manhood suffrage—without bringing Woman Suffrage
onto the cabinet table. At the time, prior to 1914, when this was
most visible Lloyd George, who might conceivably have forced
Asquith to change sides, was neutralised by the Marconi scandal. Four years later, when Suffrage matters again brought
Woman Suffrage into the arena, Asquith's position had been

seriously eroded by events and, when Lloyd George replaced him, Suffrage, in some form, was virtually certain.

Before 1914 ardent Liberal Suffragists in and out of Parliament found that their ardour had to be cooled in face of party realities. Both the National Liberal Federation and the Women's Liberal Federation were pressing for Suffrage, the latter especially desperately. Neither, however, were for it at the expense of bringing into disarray, if not destruction, a cabinet on which so many of their other hopes rested. Much as they resented the consequences of having to repress militant Suffragettes—forcible feeding, the Cat and Mouse Act and the wide unease at such illiberality—there was little, if any, suggestion that Asquith must go. The stormier the political seas after 1908 the more vital it was to give support to the captain. Asquith, then, was doubly secure in his stand on Suffrage. Not only did he wield his considerable personal and official force but events—and Liberal hopes—conspired to put serious thoughts of his removal out of the question at least until 1914.

Woman Suffrage illustrates the power of the Prime Minister over his party in the Commons and the country. It was not the power of command so much as that of persuasion exercised expediently at the fulcrum of the political system. The same social, economic and political forces which threatened cabinet unity—social welfare, industrial unrest, Ireland, national security—were the very stuff of so many hopes for that cabinet's survival. Irish as much as Labour M.P.s by 1912 had a heavy investment in the continuation of Liberal control. The Parliament Act had opened vistas of political possibility which, for many, needed prompt if careful exploitation. A general election seen from 1912 could not be delayed much beyond 1914, and the task of amassing a record of achievements to present to the electorate by that time was a feat of political management in itself. Once the Plural Voting Act was through, in the wake of the Franchise and Registration Bill débâcle, the electoral ground rules for the next election were clear. The Liberals, even so, might easily not win and it was therefore vital that they complete as much legislation as possible before 1914. In this situation Asquith's influence as chief manager was considerable. Too much was at stake for any save the most ardent Suffragist among Liberal M.P.s to question the fact that not only was Suffrage not on the agenda, but Asquith might conceivably keep it off the agenda through another election. If that happened, and if the Liberals lost, then the Tories might either ignore the matter or possibly plump for the limited enfranchisement which Disraeli had considered and which—to secure votes for *some* women—not a few Liberals would be sorely tempted to support.

That such thoughts could even be entertained is testimony of the blindness of Asquith to the needs of the party and the opportunity it had to exploit electoral opportunities. This is a reflection not on Woman Suffrage, but on the whole question of electoral reform. Such, at least, is the judgement of Dr. Clarke, commenting on the fate of the 'New Liberalism'. 'Paradoxically', he claims, the new Liberalism's failure was not over social democracy but political democracy. A fourth Reform Act was needed, yet the only terms on which it could come were by including woman suffrage. Asquith's failure to see either the necessity or the urgency of this is the most serious criticism that can be made of his leadership.'[1]

The parliamentary difficulties were considerable, but not insuperable had the principle been accepted by Asquith and a firm lead been given from the top as the Franchise Bill was being drafted, in the winter of 1911–12. There was a sufficient degree of Liberal–Labour consensus by then to have allowed opposition in cabinet and among Liberals to be overawed or nullified. The parallel passage of the Home Rule Bill would have allowed the exclusion of Ireland, thus strengthening the Nationalists' desire to help the Liberal government. In short it was clear that, by early 1912, opponents of Suffrage among Liberals, Labour, and Irish backbenchers were influential *precisely* because they knew they were exploiting a split in the cabinet and that the Prime Minister was using them against his colleagues.

[1] Clarke, P. F., *Lancashire and the New Liberalism* (Cambridge U.P., 1971), p. 399.

Asquith's 'want of imagination'[2] on Suffrage was part of a wider failure to appreciate what was potentially at stake in the area of electoral reform. Even as late as September 1916 Edwin Montagu, at least, still feared that the situation had not changed, that Asquith was ready to allow Tories like Walter Long to set the pace. Asquith's prejudice against Woman Suffrage almost certainly aggravated his myopia on electoral reform; and that, in turn, contributed to the failure of the 'New Liberalism' and the rise of the Labour party. The Suffrage campaign, seen from inside the cabinet, does not provide much evidence for the inevitability of that rise. Far from revealing the Liberal party as moribund, the response to the Suffrage campaign was one among several responses which revealed the party, generally, as capable of responding to social needs and restive under a leadership which allowed itself to be wholly concerned with other questions. In short, the Woman Suffrage campaign suggests that a failure of leadership after 1912, coupled with the distractions of non-English questions —Ireland and Welsh Disestablishment—gave the party an unfavourable image in England which the war intensified and the Labour party exploited.

THE SUFFRAGE MOVEMENT

This has not been a study of the Suffrage movement proper. It has, in effect, almost reversed the order of things described at the outset, wherein the motivations of politicians and the effects of the political system have been taken for granted in the literature that exists. Nevertheless, the views of Suffragists and their activities have featured widely in the narrative. Moreover, Suffragists and their activities were an important variable in the political equation and it would be wrong to give any other impression. In the light of political realities as they existed after 1906, what may be said of the roles of the Suffragists and Suffragettes?

To begin, it is clear that the key variable within the Suffrage

[2] Jenkins, Roy, *Asquith* (Collins, London, 1965), p. 242.

movement was the WSPU. Without its eruption into politics after 1906, the Suffrage question would not in Balfour's words, have secured a place for itself 'in the swim'.[3] Even given that a majority of Liberals were privately pledged to Suffrage, and that it was clear that Liberals must attend to franchise business, it is still most unlikely that without militancy Suffrage would have been given active cabinet consideration, far less cabinet approval. As Mrs. Fawcett herself admitted, the Pankhursts changed that situation decisively so that, by March 1908, in Asquith's first declaration on the subject, Suffrage was portrayed as a matter for the Commons to decide when the government brought in its own bill for electoral reform. This was not what the WSPU had demanded. It did, however, symbolize the recognition of the fact that it would be difficult for Liberals thereafter to deal with suffrage matters at all without dealing with Woman Suffrage, however difficult that might be for them and their leader. The disregarding by the government of Private Member's bills and the torpedoing of the Conciliation Bill, alike, testified to the WSPU conviction that on such a question a government would demand and secure its own bill or nothing. Since it could not agree on Suffrage, the latter was more likely, and that event the WSPU thought it could prevent by forcing a change of mind.

Mrs. Pankhurst and her daughters were no more adept at reading between political lines than Mrs. Fawcett. They both read the same dilemma for Liberals but reacted differently to it. Whether Mrs. Fawcett's old Liberal loyalties had an influence is not really important. The fact was that neither she nor her colleagues and followers were ready to try to force the government's hand by well-publicized protests which courted jail and later near-martyrdom. Mrs. Pankhurst brought from her more recent working-class association the more desperate, defiant flavour of lower-class activism and added her own sense of drama and immediacy. Little of either was visible in the NUWSS. Once she had initiated the cycle of protest—repression—new and stronger pro-

[3] Quoted in Christabel Pankhurst, *Unshackled. The Story of How We Won the Vote* (Hutchinson, London, 1959), p. 58.

test, the pace was set, not by the daughter who shared her Socialism, Sylvia, but by the one who increasingly did not, Christabel. The latter, as we saw, tried hard for a Tory promise of co-operation, so convinced was she that the trades unions and not the Liberals were the long-term enemy of feminists.

Can it be said that militancy delayed the coming of Suffrage? The answer is almost certainly no. The nature of the question meant, in Parliamentary terms, that the real obstacles lay elsewhere—in the Lords, among Liberals and the Irish, if not some Labour M.P.s. While it is true that militant protest forced the question out into the public arena, it is equally true that after 1910 militancy may have become relatively counter-productive. The Pankhursts had exploited the cheap press very successfully. Militancy, however, to retain its newsworthiness had to intensify its tactics fairly steadily and, by 1910, was undoubtedly losing supporters from the movement. When the Pankhursts took to guerrilla war on property and engaged in arson, then their behaviour had long gone past the tolerance of the man on the Clapham omnibus—though it might be argued by Suffragettes that many such men were threatening such things in the long hot summer of Edwardian industrial ferment. Certainly, so far as can be seen, Mrs. Pankhurst hurt the cause among M.P.s and made Asquith's position easier after the Franchise Bill had been announced. The arrest for conspiracy of the Pankhursts and Pethick-Lawrences was, after all, accompanied by general parliamentary acclaim. Nevertheless it seemed reasonably clear that Asquith had no intention of including Suffrage in the Franchise Bill and, if the question had come to a vote, Tories, Liberal dissidents, and the Irish would have killed it for reasons other than the behaviour of militants. Once Christabel—who had escaped to Paris—sanctioned the destruction of property, she faced two related problems. The first concerned overall control—could she prevent Suffrage becoming just a cover for any unbalanced individual? Secondly, sooner or later, was not the campaign going to lead to a loss of life? In the event neither occurred; but this cannot be laid solely at the door of WSPU precautions.

What of the non-militant Suffragists? Their role was, in effect, to exploit the opening the WSPU had made. Deploring militancy, they used it to argue for the necessity of Suffrage to prevent a bad situation becoming worse. Soothing affronted politicians, they yet kept up a barrage of persuasion which penetrated sensibilities shaken out of their complacent ignorance. Above all, they *organized* themselves, so that by 1912 Liberals who were anti Suffrage feared their electoral interventions, and the Labour Representation Committee welcomed their promise of *organized* help at the coming election. At the outbreak of war the Pankhursts went quickly off into bellicose chauvinism—with the exception of Sylvia of course. Mrs. Fawcett, as we saw, resisted her pacifist and anti-war followers and led the NUWSS off into war work, a fact which was allowed to escape no one's notice and proved to be a useful political credit after 1916.

The Woman Suffrage campaign, and the militant Suffragettes in particular, shocked Edwardian England and contributed markedly to the hysteria which many observers, domestic and foreign, saw as one of the hallmarks of the years after 1909. The effusions of Christabel Pankhurst on the one hand, and those of someone like Sir Almroth Wright on the other, were evidence that the campaign tapped highly dangerous sources of deep and concealed resentments. A final judgement, however, must take in a great deal more than surface impressions. It must take note of the steady mobilization of women after 1900, not just for the vote, but for much greater opportunities in school and later at work and, not least, for much greater individual freedom.

What was happening—much too slowly for feminists of course —was a slow but profound change in the self-image held by women. Within the family situation, knowledge of methods of birth control were spreading the possibilities of a life less dominated by large numbers of children. Biological research had destroyed two widespread, if contradictory beliefs, namely that women provided merely an environment for a male-produced embryo and, secondly, that the female determined the sex of children.[4] In consequence women began to find their half share in their children's inheritance recognized, and were freed from the old cross of guilt for failure to give their husbands sons. Dangerfield was on safe ground in highlighting these profound changes and their effects—even if neither Pankhurst daughter was an adequate symbol either of the present or future political or social allegiances of the mass of women.

The strenuous opposition of the government after 1906 helped quicken the mobilization of women and the process of changing their image of themselves. The effect of the war was to speed both processes still further. Asquith's opposition could then be said to have been not without value to the feminist cause, hard though it almost certainly was on the Liberal cause in England. Dangerfield was correct in seeing the Pankhursts as symbols of a new and ultimately irresistible force; but he was wrong to see the Liberal party as an immovable object or (as it proved) 'Liberal England' as dependent on the survival of the Liberal party.

[4] The former is identified with the work of Hertwig, Fol and Van Berenden; the latter with the names of Doncaster, Raynor, Corres, Dunham and Marryot after 1906. See F. A. E. Grew, *Sex Determination* (Methuen, London, 1965), pp. 3–10 and F. J. Cole, *Early Theories of Sexual Generation* (Oxford U.P., 1930), p. 186 et. seq.

Bibliography

UNPRINTED SOURCES

(Unless otherwise stated, the Papers below may be seen at the British Museum)

A. *Suffragists and Suffrage Organizations*
1. The Papers of the Women's Social and Political Union, at the London Museum.
2. The Papers of Dame Millicent Garrett Fawcett, comprising the Women's Service Library Autograph Collection on Woman Suffrage at the Fawcett Society Library.

B. *The Prime Minister and Cabinet*
1. The Papers of Augustine Birrell at the Harold Cohen Library, University of Liverpool.
2. The Papers of John Burns.
3. The Papers of Sir Henry Campbell-Bannerman.
4. The Papers of the Marquess of Crewe at the University Library, Cambridge.
5. The Papers of Herbert, Viscount Gladstone.
6. The Papers of Edward, Viscount Grey of Falloden at the Public Record Office.
7. The Papers of Richard, Viscount Haldane of Cloan at the National Library of Scotland.
8. The Papers of Lewis, Viscount Harcourt at the Bodleian Library, Oxford.
9. The Papers of Earl Lloyd George of Dwyfor at the Beaverbrook Library, London.

10. The Papers of Reginald McKenna at the Library, Churchill College, Cambridge.
11. The Papers of Henry, 1st Earl of Oxford and Asquith at the Bodleian Library, Oxford.
12. The Papers of Walter, 1st Viscount Runciman at the Library, University of Newcastle-Upon-Tyne.
13. The Papers of Herbert, Viscount Samuel at the House of Lords Record Office.

C. Other Collections

1. The Papers of Arthur, 1st Earl of Balfour.
2. The Papers of Lord Robert Cecil.
3. The Papers of Austen Chamberlain at the Library, University of Birmingham.
4. The Papers of A. Bonar Law at the Beaverbrook Library, London.
5. The Papers of George Lansbury at the British Library of Political and Economic Science.
6. The Papers of Alexander Murray, 1st Baron Elibank at the National Library of Scotland.
7. The Papers of William O'Brien at the National Library of Ireland, Dublin.
8. The Papers of John Redmond at the National Library of Ireland, Dublin.
9. The Papers of C. P. Scott.
10. The Papers of Sidney and Beatrice Webb, Baron and Baroness Passfield, at the British Library of Political and Economic Science.

D. Political Parties

1. The Independent Labour Party. Minutes of the City of London Branch, 1906–16, in 3 Volumes. Minutes of the Divisional Council No. 6, 1909–16. Both at the British Library of Political and Economic Science.
2. The Labour Party: Minutes, Letters and other Papers en-

titled '*The Infancy of Labour*' 1900–18, 2 Volumes. At the British Library of Political and Economic Science.

3. The Liberal Party

   (a) Bradford Liberal Association, General Council, Minutes 1911–18. At Liberal Party Offices, Bradford.

   (b) Yorkshire Liberal Federation, General Council, Minutes 1902–21.

   (c) Yorkshire Women's Liberal Federation, Executive Committee, Minutes, 1911–18.

   (d) Society of Certified and Associated Liberal Agents, Minutes of the Council 1909–15.

   Parts (b) (c) (d) held at Liberal Party Offices at Leeds.

   (e) Women's Liberal Federation, National Executive Committee, Minutes, June 1910–July 1912.

PRINTED SOURCES

1. PARLIAMENTARY REPORTS 1905–18

2. THE PRESS

    The Times
    Morning Post
    Daily Chronicle
    Manchester Guardian
    Daily News and Leader
    Pall Mall Gazette

3. SUFFRAGE PAMPHLETS

A. *National Union of Woman Suffrage Societies Publications*

   1. Annual Reports 1905–19
   2. Newspaper, *The Common Cause* 1909–18
   3. Pamphlets: (i) author given

   Brailsford, H. N., 'Women and The Reform Bill' (December 1911).

Brailsford, H. N., 'Women and The Reform Bill' (July 1912).

Fawcett, Mrs. Henry, 'The Representation of the People Bill in the House of Lords. A Plea for Peace' (1917).

Ring, F. C., 'Women's Suffrage and Temperance' (May 1913).

Robertson, Margaret, 'Working Men and Woman Suffrage' (November 1912).

Royden, M., 'Speech of Miss M. Royden at the Albert Hall' (February 1914).

(ii) Pamphlets—no author or editor given

'The New Development in the Policy of the N.U.W.S.S.'.

'Women's Suffrage: A Survey 1908–12'.

'The Vital Claim. An Appeal from Liberal Women to Women Liberals'.

'The Labour Party and the Reform Bill' (December 1912).

'The Position of the N.U.W.S.S.' (February 1913).

'What is the Active Service League?' (May 1914).

'The All-British Lightning Campaign' (May 1914).

'The Account of the Deputation to the Prime Minister', 8 August 1913.

'A Brief Review of the Women's Suffrage Movement Since its Beginning in 1832' (September 1913).

B. *Women's Social and Political Union Publications*

1. Annual Conference Reports 1905–7
2. Newspapers
   Votes for Women 1907–18.
   The Suffragette 1912–15.
   Britannia 1915–18.

C. *Women's Freedom League Publications*

Annual Reports 1907–19

D. *Northern Men's Federation for Women's Suffrage Publications*

(i) Pamphlets

Sennet, Mrs. Arncliffe, 'Make Way for the Prime Minister' (1912).

Sennet, Mrs. Arncliffe, 'Women's Suffrage and Parliamentary Morals' (December 1910).

(ii) Pamphlets—no author or editor given

'Deputation at Berwick to Sir Edward Grey', 22 November 1913.

E. *Women's Liberal Federation Publications*

(i) Pamphlets

Bamford Slack (no title), (July 1903).

Carlisle, Countess of, 'Appeal to the Women's Liberal Federation' (July 1895).

McLaren, Mrs. Eva, 'The History of the Women's Suffrage Movement in the Women's Liberal Federation' (April 1903).

Trevelyan, Lady (no title), (November 1901).

(ii) Pamphlets—no author or editor given

'Mr. Lloyd George on Woman's Suffrage at the Albert Hall' (5 December, 1908).

'Mr. Lloyd George on Woman's Suffrage' (September 1913).

'What Shall We Do Next?' (1914).

F. *Conservative and Unionist Women's Franchise Association Publications*

(i) Pamphlets

Chance, Lady, 'Words to Working Women on Woman Suffrage' (July 1912).

Chance, Lady, 'The Predominance of Men in the Anti Suffrage Finance and Organisation'.

Grant, J. C., 'Women Suffrage: Its History and Constitutional Aspect'.

(ii) Pamphlets—no author or editor given

Earl of Selborne: 'Address at the Hotel Cecil on 9 March 1911'.

'Debate on Woman Suffrage: Lord Lytton *v.* Miss Gladys Pitt at the Temperance Hall, Birmingham, 21 October 1913'.

'Woman Suffrage in the Working. Answers From America, May 1914'.

'Impartial Enquiry Into the Effects of Woman Suffrage in Australia and New Zealand' (1914).

G. *Miscellaneous Publications*

(i) Hobhouse, T., 'Government by the People' (People's Suffrage Federation).

Lowndes, Mary, 'A B C of Politics for Women Politicians' (Artists Suffrage League, London, 1909).

Simon, Sir John, 'Speeches to the National Delegates Meeting 4 December, 1912' (The Woman's Suffrage Campaign).

(ii) Miscellaneous—no publisher

Fawcett, M. G., 'The Speakers Conference on Electoral Reform'.

Ponsonby, Arthur, M.P., 'The Opportunity of 1912'.

Shaw, F. J., 'Women's Votes and Party Tactics' (1909).

Snowden, Philip, M.P., 'In Defence of the Conciliation Bill' (Printed at Rydal Press, Keighley, 1911).

Snowden, Philip, M.P., 'The Dominant Issue'.

Snowden, Philip, M.P., 'The Present Position of Woman Suffrage' (December 1913).

(iii) Miscellaneous—no author

'The Conciliation Committee for Woman Suffrage'.

'Woman Municipal Electors and the Parliamentary Vote' (1911).

'Mr. Birrell's Reply to the Anti-Suffrage Delegation' (a report from the Western Daily Press, Bristol, 26 February 1912).

4. ARTICLES

Adams, W. S., 'Lloyd George and the Labour Movement', *Past and Present*, Number 3, February 1953, pp. 55–62.

'M.A.', 'The Economic Foundations of the Women's Movement', *Fabian Tract No. 175*, July 1914.

Blewett, Neal, 'Free Fooders, Balfourites, Whole Hoggers. Factionalism within the Unionist Party 1906–10', *History Journal*, Vol. XI, No. 1 (1968), pp. 95–124.

Boyd, F. M., 'Palliatives, Politics and the Socialist Vote', *Social Democracy*, Volume 14, No. 6, 15 June 1910, pp. 259–64.

Clarke, A. H., 'Marriage with Deceased Wife's Sister and the Cry of Disestablishment', *The Nineteenth Century*, Volume 67, No. 396. February 1910, pp. 257–72.

Cook, Lady (Tennessee Claflin), 'Who Rules?', *Socal Democracy*, Volume 14, No. 4, 15 April 1910, pp. 173–5.

Cox, Harold, 'The Possibility of Compromise', *The Nineteenth Century*, Volume 67, No. 399, May 1910, pp. 786–92.

David, Edward, 'The Liberal Party Divided 1916–18', *History Journal*, Vol. XIII, No. 3 (1970), pp. 509–32.

Dicey, A. V., 'On the Brink of an Abyss', *The Nineteenth Century*, Volume 67, No. 399, May 1910, pp. 779–85.

Dunraven, Lord, 'The Constitutional "Sham Fight" ', *The Nineteenth Century*, Volume 67, No. 399, May 1910, pp. 765–78.

Fawcett, M. G., 'War and Reconstruction—Women and Their Use of the Vote', *The English Review*, February 1918, pp. 260–6.

Hunter, E. H., 'In Days of Change', *Social Democracy*, Volume 14, No. 6, 15 June 1910, pp. 241–6.

Kenney, Roland, 'Women's Suffrage', *The English Review*, December 1912, pp. 98–108.

Mallett, C. E., 'Woman Suffrage and the Liberal Party', *The Nineteenth Century*, Volume 71, No. 421, March 1912, pp. 599–608.

Marriet, J. A. R., 'Reform of the House of Lords', *The Nineteenth Century*, Volume 65, No. 383, January 1909, pp. 34–47.

Massingham, H. W., 'The Position of Mr. Lloyd George', *The Nation*, Volume 10, No. 14, 6 January, 1912, pp. 578–9.

Massingham, H. W., 'The Task of the Prime Minister', *The Nation*, Volume 10, No. 17, 27 January 1912, pp. 687–9.

Morgan, K. O., 'Lloyd George's Premiership. A Study in Prime Ministerial Government', *History Journal*, Vol. XIII, No. 1 (1970).

Morgan, K. O., 'Asquith as Prime Minister 1908–16', *English Historical Review*, Vol. LXXXV (1970) pp. 502–31.

Quelch, Harry, 'Social Democracy and Ladies Suffrage', *Social Democracy*, Volume 14, No. 7. 15 July 1910, pp. 289–94.

Ribblesdale, Lord, 'The Constitutional "Crisis" ', *The Nineteenth Century*, Volume 67, No. 399, May 1910, pp. 793–7.

Samuels, H. B., 'Woman Suffrage', *Social Democracy*, Volume 2, No. 14, 15 February 1910, pp. 69–72.

Schloesser, Henry H., 'The Twentieth Century Reform Bill', *Fabian Society Tract No. 153*, January 1911.

Seton-Kerr, Henry, 'The Radical Party and Social Reform', *The Nineteenth Century*, Volume 68, No. 406, December 1910, pp. 1119–23.

Weston, Corinne, 'The Liberal Leadership and the Lords Veto 1907–10', *History Journal*, Vol. XI, No. 3 (1968), 508–37.

Woods, H. L., 'Woman Suffrage Not a Sex Question', *Social Democracy*, Volume 14, No. 1, 15 January 1910, pp. 9–17.

Zangwill, Israel, 'The Militant Suffragists', *The English Review*, November 1913, pp. 561–77.

Unsigned Articles

'A Compromise on Woman Suffrage', *The Nation*, Volume 7, No. 9, 28 May 1910. pp. 303–4.

'Parliament and the Women's Bill', *The Nation*, Volume 9, No. 6, 1911, pp. 190–1.

'Manhood or Adult Suffrage', *The Nation*, Volume 10, No. 6, 11 November 1911, p. 225.

'Towards Adult Suffrage', *The Nation*, Volume 10, No. 9, 2 December 1911, pp. 367–9.

'The Government's Threefold Task', *The Nation*, Volume 10, No. 13, 30 December 1911, pp. 538–9.

'The Evasion of Woman Suffrage', *The Nation*, Volume 10, No. 16, 20 January 1912, pp. 646–8.

'The Prospects for Woman Suffrage', *The Nation*, Volume 10, No. 22, 2 March 1912, pp. 875–6.

'The Reform Bill and Woman Suffrage', *The Nation*, Volume 11, No. 12, 22 June 1912, pp. 424–5.

'The Irish Party and Woman Suffrage', *The Nation*, Volume 12, No. 6, 9 November 1912, p. 244.

'The Chances for Woman Suffrage', *The Nation*, Volume 12, No. 15, 11 January 1913, pp. 626–7.

'A Proposal for Woman Suffrage', *The Nation*, Volume 12, No. 22, 1 March 1913, pp. 876–87.

'Social Order and the Suffrage', *The Nation*, Volume 13, No. 6, 10 May 1913, pp. 218–19.

'Mr. Asquith and Woman Suffrage', *The Nation*, Volume 13, No. 20, 16 August 1913, pp. 738–9.

5. BOOKS—SELECT BIBLIOGRAPHY

A. Books by Suffragists, or on Suffragists or Suffrage organizations.

Balfour, Lady Betty, *ed. Letters of Constance Lytton* (William Heinemann, London 1925).

Balfour, Lady Frances, *Ne Obliviscaris* (Hodder and Stoughton, London, 1930).

Beard, Mary, *Woman as Force in History. A Study in Traditions and Realities* (Collier Books, New York, 1946).

Billington-Greig, Mrs. T. *The Militant Suffrage Movement* (Frank Palmer, London, 1912).

Blease, Walter Lyon, *The Emancipation of English Women*, (David Nutt, London, 1963).

Brittain, Vera, *Pethick-Lawrence. A Portrait* (George Allen and Unwin, London, 1963).

Bibliography

Brittain, Vera, *Lady into Woman* (Andrew Dakers, London, 1953).

Fawcett, Millicent G., *The Women's Victory—and After: Personal Reminiscences 1911–18* (Sidgwick and Jackson, London, 1920).

Fawcett, Millicent G., *What I Remember* (T. Fisher Unwin, London, 1925).

Fawcett, Millicent G., *Women's Suffrage: A Short History of a Great Movement* (The People's Books, London, 1912).

Fulford, Roger, *Votes for Women* (Faber and Faber, London, 1957).

Gardiner, A. G., *Prophets, Priests and Kings* (Alstan Rivers, London, 1908).

Gardiner, A. G., *Portraits and Portents* (Harper and Brothers, New York, 1926).

Henley, Dorothy, *Rosalind Howard, Countess of Carlisle* (Hogarth Press, London, 1958).

Kenney, Annie, *Memoirs of a Militant* (Edward Arnold, London, 1924).

Lyton, Constance, *Prisons and Prisoners* (Heinemann, London, 1914).

Mannin, Ethel, *Woman and the Revolution* (Secker and Warburg, London, 1938).

Metcalfe, A. E., *Woman's Effort* (Basil Blackwell, Oxford, 1917).

Mitchell, David, *The Fighting Pankhursts. A Study in Tenacity* (Jonathan Cape, London, 1967).

Montefiore, Dora, *From a Victorian to a Modern* (E. Archer, London, 1927).

O'Connor, Lillian, *Pioneer Women Orators* (Columbia U.P., New York, 1954).

Pankhurst, Christabel, *Unshackled: The Story of How We Won the Vote* (Hutchinson, London, 1959).

Pankhurst, Emmeline, *My Own Story* (Eveleigh Nash, London, 1914).

Pankhurst, Sylvia, *The Suffragette* (Sturgis Walton, New York, 1911).

Pankhurst, Sylvia, *The Life of Emmeline Pankhurst* (T. Werner Laurie, London, 1935).

Pankhurst, Sylvia, *The Suffrage Movement* (Longmans Green, London, 1931).

Pentland, Marjorie, *A Bonnie Fechter. Life of the Marchioness of Aberdeen* (Batsford, London, 1952).

Pethick-Lawrence, Frederick W., *Fate Has Been Kind* (Hutchinson, London, 1942).

Pethick-Lawrence, Emmeline, *My Part in a Changing World* (Gollancz, London, 1938).

Ramelson, Marion, *The Petticoat Rebellion. A Century of Struggle for Women's Rights* (Lawrence and Wishart, London, 1967).

Roberts, Charles, *The Radical Countess. The History of The Life of Rosalind, Countess of Carlisle* (Steel Brothers, Carlisle, 1962).

Rover, Constance, *Women's Suffrage and Party Politics in Britain 1866–1914* (Routledge and Kegan Paul, London, 1967).

Snowden, Ethel, *The Feminist Movement* (Collins, London, 1913).

Strachey, Ray, *The Cause* (Bell and Sons, London, 1928).

Strachey, Mrs. Ray, *Millicent Garret Fawcett* (John Murray, London, 1931).

Stenton, Doris M., *The English Woman in History* (George Allen and Unwin, London, 1957).

Swanwick, Helen M., *The Future of the Women's Movement* (Bell and Sons, London, 1913).

Thompson, William *An Appeal on behalf of one half of the human race, women, against the pretensions of the other half, men, to retain them in political and thence in civil and domestic slavery* (Longmans, Hurst Rees, London, 1825).

Wollstonecraft, Mary, *A Vindication of the Rights of Women* (Walter Scott, London, 1891).

B. *Memoirs, Biographies, and Studies*

(i) Of direct participants in the political campaign.

Balfour, A. J., *Aspects of Home Rule* (George Routledge, London, 1912).

Beaverbrook, Lord, *Politicians and the War* (Land Publications, London, Volume I, 1928, Volume II, 1932).

Beaverbrook, Lord, *Men and Power 1917–18* (Hutchinson, London, 1956).

Birkenhead, Lord, *'F.E.'* (Eyre and Spottiswoode, London, 1959).

Blake, Robert, *The Unknown Prime Minister* (Eyre and Spottiswoode, London, 1955).

Bonham-Carter, Lady Violet, *Winston Churchill. As I Knew Him* (Eyre and Spottiswoode and Collins, London, 1965).

Bowle, John, *Viscount Samuel* (Gollancz, London, 1957).

Brett, Maurice, V., *Ed., The Journal and Letters of Reginald, Viscount Esher* (Ivor Nicholson and Watson, London, 4 Vols., 1934–8).

Churchill, Randolph S., *Winston S. Churchill, Young Statesman 1901–14* (Heinemann, London, 1966), Vol. II of the biography of Winston S. Churchill.

Chamberlain, Sir Austen, *Down the Years* (Cassell, London, 1935).

Chamberlain, Sir Austen, *Politics From Inside* (Cassell, London, 1936).

Cole, G. D. H., *John Burns* (Gollancz, London, 1943).

Cole, M. *Ed., Beatrice Webb's Diaries 1912–1924* (Longmans Green, London, 1952).

Driberg, Tom, *Beaverbrook* (Weidenfeld and Nicolson, London, 1956).

Dugdale, Mrs. Edgar, *Arthur James Balfour* (Hutchinson, London, 1936, 2 Vols.).

Edwards, J. H., *David Lloyd George* (Waverley Book Company, London, 4 Vols., 1913, 2 Vols., 1930).

Elton, Lord, *The Life of J. Ramsey MacDonald* (Collins, London, 1939).

George, Richard Lloyd, *Lloyd George* (Frederick Muller, London, 1960).

Gladstone, Herbert, *After Thirty Years* (Hutchinson, London, 1932).

Gwynn, Denis, *The Life of John Redmond* (Harrap, London, 1932).

Haldane, Richard B., *An Autobiography* (Hodder and Stoughton, London, 1929).

Hamilton, Mary Agnes, *Arthur Henderson* (Heinemann, London, 1938).

Hammond, J. E., *C. P. Scott* (Bell and Sons, London, 1934).

Harris, Wilson, *J. A. Spender* (Cassell, London, 1946).

Healy, T. M., *Letters and Leaders Of My Day* (Thornton Butterworth, London, 1928), 2 Vols.

Hughes, Emrys, *Keir Hardie* (George Allen and Unwin, London, 1956).

Hyde, H. M., *Carson. The Life of Sir Edward Carson, Lord Carson of Duncairn* (Heinemann, London, 1953).

Jenkins, Roy, *Mr. Balfour's Poodle* (Heinemann, London, 1954).

Jenkins, Roy, *Sir Charles Dilke* (Collins, London, 1958).

Jenkins, Roy, *Asquith* (Collins, London, 1965).

Jones, Jack, *The Man David 1880–1914* (Hamish Hamilton, London, 1944).

Jones, Thomas, *Lloyd George* (Oxford, U.P., Oxford, 1951).

Koss, Stephen E., *Lord Haldane. Scapegoat for Liberalism* (Columbia U.P., New York, 1969).

Kent, William, *John Burns, Labour's Lost Leader* (Williams and Norgate, London, 1950).

Lansbury, George, *My Life* (Constable, London, 1928).

Long, Viscount Walter of Wraxall, *Memories* (Hutchinson, London, 1923).

Mallett, Sir Charles, *Mr. Lloyd George. A Study* (Benn, London, 1930).

Mallet, Sir Charles, *Herbert Gladstone. A Memoir* (Hutchinson, London, 1932).

Masterman, Lucy, *C. F. G. Masterman, A Biography* (Nicholson and Watson, London, 1939).

Maurice, Sir Frank, *Haldane 1856–1915* (Faber and Faber, London, 1937).

McKenna, Stephen, *Reginald McKenna* (Eyre and Spottiswoode, London, 1948).

Morgan, John H., *John, Viscount Morley* (John Murray, London, 1924).

Morley, John, Lord, *Recollections* (Macmillan, London, 1917), 2 Vols.

Murray, Basil, *'L.G.'* (Sampson Low, London, 1933).

Newton, Thomas Legh, Lord, *Lord Lansdowne* (Macmillan, London, 1929).

Newton, Thomas Legh, Lord, *Retrospection* (John Murray, London, 1941).

Nicolson, Harold, *King George The Fifth. His Life and Reign* (Constable, London, 1953).

O'Connor, T. P., *Memoirs of An Old Parliamentarian* (Ernest Benn, London, 1929).

Oxford and Asquith, Countess of, *The Autobiography of Margot Asquith* (Thornton Butterworth, London, 1922), 2 Vols.

Oxford and Asquith, Countess of, *More Memories* (Cassell, London, 1933).

Oxford and Asquith, Countess of, *Off the Record* (Frederick Muller, London, 1943).

Oxford and Asquith, Earl of, *Fifty Years of Parliament* (Cassell, London, 1926), 2 Vols.

Oxford and Asquith, Earl of, *Memories and Reflections 1852–1927* (Cassell, London, 1928), 2 Vols.

Oxford and Asquith, Earl of, *Speeches By The Earl of Oxford and Asquith K.G.* (Hutchinson, London, 1928).

Petrie, Sir Charles, *Walter Long and His Times* (Hutchinson, London, 1936).

Petrie, Sir Charles, *The Life and Letters of The Rt. Hon. Sir Austen Chamberlain* (Cassell, London 1939), 2 Vols.

Pope-Hennessy, James, *Lord Crewe, The Likeness of a Liberal* (Constable, London, 1955).

Postgate, Raymond, *The Life of George Lansbury* (Longmans Green and Co., London, 1951).

Raymond, E. T., *Mr. Lloyd George* (Collins, London, 1922).

Reading, The Marquess of, *Rufus Isaacs, First Marquess of Reading* (Hutchinson, London, 1945).

Riddell, Lord, *War Diary 1914–18*, (Ivor Nicholson and Watson, London, 1933).

Riddell, Lord, *More Pages From My Diary, 1908–14* (Country Life, London, 1934).

Roberts, Bechhoffer, *Sir John Simon* (Robert Hale, London, 1938).

Ronaldshay, Earl of, *The Life of Lord Curzon* (Ernest Benn, London, 1928), 3 Vols.

Samuel, Lord, *Memoirs* (The Cresset Press, London, 1945).

Smith, F. E., *Law, Life and Letters* (Hodder and Stoughton, London, 1927), 2 Vols.

Smith, F. E., *The Speeches of Lord Birkenhead* (Cassell, London, 1929).

Snowden, Philip, *An Autobiography of Philip, Viscount Snowden* (Ivor Nicholson and Watson, London, 1934), Vol. I.

Sommer, Dudley, *Haldane of Cloan* (George Allen and Unwin, London, 1960).

Spender, J. A., and Asquith, Cyril, *The Life of Herbert Henry Asquith, Lord Oxford and Asquith* (Hutchinson, London, 1932), 2 Vols.

Spender, J. A., *The Life of Sir Hubert Campbell-Bannerman* (Hodder and Stoughton, London, 1923).

Stewart, W., *J. Keir Hardie* (I.L.P. Pub. Department, London, 1925).

Taylor, A. J. P., *Ed.*—Stevenson, Frances, *Lloyd George. A Diary* (Hutchinson, London, 1971).

Bibliography

Thompson, Malcolm, *David Lloyd George* (Hutchinson, London, 1948).

Trevelyan, G. M., *Grey of Fallodon* (Longmans Green, London, 1937).

Ullswater, Viscount James Lowther of, *A Speaker's Commentaries* (Edward Arnold, London, 1925), 2 Vols.

White, Hope C., *Willoughby Hyett Dickinson: A Memoir* (John Bellows, Gloucester, 1956).

Wilson, John C. B., *A Life of Sir Henry Campbell-Bannerman* (Constable, London, 1973).

Young, Kenneth, *Arthur James Balfour* (Bell and Sons, London, 1963).

(ii) Of others.

Amery, Julian, *Life of Joseph Chamberlain* (Macmillan, London, Vol. IV, 1951).

Bell, G. K. A., *Randall Davidson* (Oxford U.P., Oxford, 1935), 2 Vols.

Crewe-Milnes, The Marquis Quentin, *The Marquis of Rosebery* (John Murray, London, 1931), 2 Vols.

Fitzroy, Sir Almeric, *Memoirs* (Hutchinson, London, 1925), 2 Vols.

Fox, Mrs. A. Wilson, *The Earl of Halsbury* (Chapman and Hall, London, 1929).

Gollin, A. M., *The Observer and J. L. Garvin 1908–14* (Oxford U.P., Oxford, 1960).

James, Robert V. Rhodes, *Rosebery* (Weidenfeld and Nicolson, London, 1963).

Macdonagh, Michael, *The Life of William O'Brien; the Irish Nationalist* (Ernest Benn, London, 1928).

Pankhurst, R. K. P., *William Thompson* (Watts, London, 1954).

Trevelyan, Janet P., *The Life of Mrs. Humphrey Ward* (Constable, London, 1934).

Ward, Mrs. Humphrey, *A Writer's Recollections* (Collins, London, 1918).

Webb, Beatrice, *My Apprenticeship* (Longmans Green and Co., London, 1950).

Wedgewood, C. V., *The Last of The Radicals* (Jonathan Cape, London, 1951).

Wedgewood, Josiah C., *Memoirs of a Fighting Life* (Hutchinson, London, 1941).

C. General and Miscellaneous Works

Banks, J. A., and Banks, O., *Feminism and Family Planning in Victorian England* (Liverpool U.P., Liverpool, 1964).

Bax, E. Belfort, *The Fraud of Feminism* (Grant Richards, Ltd., London, 1913).

Bealey, F., and Pelling, H., *Labour and Politics, 1900–06* (Macmillan, London, 1958).

Bebel, A., *Women and Socialism* (Trans. by Daniel DeLeon) (New York 1904).

Beer, Samuel H., *Modern British Politics, A Study of Parties and Pressure Groups* (Faber and Faber, London, 1965).

Blewett, N., *The Peers, the Party and the People. The General Elections of 1920* (Macmillan, London, 1970).

Burrow, J. W., *Evolution and Society. A Study in Victorian Social Theory* (Cambridge U.P., 1966).

Clarke, P. F., *Lancashire and the New Liberalism* (Cambridge U.P., 1971).

Clegg, H. A., Fox, A., Thompson, A. F., *A History of British Trade Unions Since 1889,* Vol. I (Clarendon Press, Oxford, 1964).

Cole, F. J., *Early Theories of Sexual Generation* (Clarendon Press, Oxford, 1930).

Dangerfield, George, *The Strange Death of Liberal England* (Paladin, London, 1966).

Emy, H. V., *Liberals, Radicals and Social Politics 1892–1914* (Cambridge U.P., 1973).

Ensor, R. C. K., *England 1870–1914* (Oxford History of England, Clarendon Press, Oxford, 15 Vols, Vol. XIV, 1952).

Bibliography

Grew, F. A. E., *Sex Determination* (Methuen, London, 1965).

Halevy, Elie, *A History of the English People in the Nineteenth Century* (Ernest Benn, London, 1952), Volume 6, Parts 1 and 2.

Hutchins, B. I., *Women in Modern History* (G. Bell and Sons, London, 1915).

Kamm, Josephine, *Hope Deferred* (Methuen, London, 1965).

Matthew, H. C. G., *The Liberal Imperialists. The ideas and politics of a post-Gladstonian élite* (Oxford U.P., 1973).

Mill, J. S., 'The Subjection of Women' in *Three Essays by John Stuart Mill* (Oxford U.P., 1963).

Mitchell, B. R., and Deane, P., *Abstract of British Historical Statistics* (Cambridge U.P., 1962).

Wright, Sir Almroth, *The Unexpurgated Case Against Women's Suffrage* (Constable, London, 1913).

Index

Index

Davison, Emily W. 125
Deceased Wife's Sister Act 1907 46
Derby, Lord 27
DeSousa *v.* Cobden 16n.
Dickinson, W. H. 45, 123, 129
Dilke, Sir Charles 42
Disraeli, Benjamin 12, 13, 38
Dublin 1
Durham, Earl of 116

East End Federation of Women's Suffrage Societies 131–2, 153
Education Act 1902 31
Edward, H.M. King 41
Elibank, Master of 67, 79, 82, 89, 99, 104, 132
Ellis, Mrs. William 10
Elmy, Mrs. Wolstenholme 16
Emy, H. V. 13, 25–7, 41
Englishwomen's Journal 11
Ensor, R. C. K. 4, 24, 40

Fabian Women's Group 97
Fawcett, Henry 13
Fawcett, Mrs. Millicent 2, 14, 44, 49, 50, 54, 89, 92, 99, 103, 125, 128, 135–6, 139, 145, 159, 161
Fawcett Society 2
Forsyth, William 13
Fouche, Mrs. 145
Franchise and Registration Bill 1912 102, 122, 152
Fulford, Roger 1

Galsworthy, John 106
Gardiner, A. G. 81
Garrison, William Lloyd 16
Geake, Charles 35, 73
Gladstone, Herbert 1, 27, 35, 41, 43, 49, 52, 56, 59, 60–1, 81, 103, 121, 123, 151
Gladstone, W. E. 12, 13, 25, 30, 36–7
Glasier, Mrs. Bruce 129
Godwin, William 9

Governesses' Benevolent Institute 11
Grey, Sir Edward 16, 37, 41, 59, 60, 69, 75, 86, 88, 90, 96, 116–17, 124, 127, 130, 134

Haldane, Elizabeth 84
Haldane, R. B. 10, 41, 74–5, 108, 137
Halevy, Elie 4
Halsbury, Lord 76
Harcourt, Lewis 41, 64, 90, 95–6, 105, 113, 118, 153
Harcourt, Sir William 24, 35
Hardie, Keir 29, 33, 42, 44, 46, 114
Hartington, Lord 27
Healy, Timothy 147–8
Henderson, Arthur 29, 67, 85, 92, 134, 137–9, 144
Herbert, Jesse 70
Hobhouse, Charles 92
Hughes, Tom 12
Hunt, Orator 10
Hutchins, B. L. 21

Independent Labour Party 16, 29, 33–4, 129
International Council of Women 18, 19
International Woman Suffrage Association 135–6

Jersey, Lady 58
Johnson, Miss Amy 96
Joicey, Lord 116

Kamm, Josephine 19
Kenney, Annie 62
Knollys, Lord 83

Labouchere, Henry 12
Lansbury, George 106–8
Lansdowne, Lord 76, 78
Licensing Act 1904 31
Lloyd George, David 1, 7, 41, 52, 56, 69, 76, 79, 82–9, 90–1, 94–6,

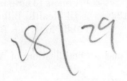